FOREWORD BY
NEW YORK TIMES BESTSELLING AUTHOR,
RAYMOND AARON

I0086522

A BOOK ON THE JOYS OF SELF DISCOVERY

Vivian Baak

WWW.FINDPEACEANDHEAL.COM

ISBN: 978-1-77277-204-3
PUBLISHED BY:
10-10-10 PUBLISHING
MARKHAM, ON
CANADA

find peace and *heal*

A book on the joys of Self discovery

DEDICATION

Having seen you
I am the Joy
your light soaked through the thickened fog
of my sunset

Seagulls caress
dancing with the wind
tousled your hair,
calls out announcing to me your shore

I saw you
Firm
Loyal
Immovable

Where I'd thought Me to be a
shaken sail,
beat down in your gaze
I discover myself as sailboat

Drawn to you
as South to North,
I stopped still
anchored at long last
in your bay of peace
I am nurtured

And ending your night-shift
you gift me the dawn

I Awaken!
knowing now how
I am The Sea

For my Beacon, Cristian

FOREWORD

You may feel a desire to awaken to higher consciousness. Perhaps it is something you have searched for and have even been learning about for quite some time. Whether or not you are already on the path to discovering your purpose in life, or just starting out to find meaning, this book is for you. Within these pages you will find honest content that can help you progress in your own processes to find yourself, and this is what Vivian has been able to decode for you in every chapter.

Find Peace and Heal is a tale of awakening, in which you will see yourself reflected in the same situations the author has experienced in her path to finding inner peace, joy and as a result, healing. She shows a simple way to find your purpose in life remembering what you used to dream about when you were a child; recover your real nature of joy as you reconnect with that purpose and evolve to a life of meaning healing others as you heal yourself physically, emotionally and spiritually.

Using stories from her own experience as well as what she has learned from her own mentors, *Vivian* also teaches you how to change every situation and the world around you by first changing yourself; how trying to control everything in your life has driven you away from the flow of life that can heal you and your relationships with others; and how acceptance is the key to open the door to joy in your life.

Raymond Aaron
New York Times Bestselling Author

A LETTER TO DEEPAK CHOPRA

I compare the moment we wake up, to the day when a bird is born. The first person we see, will always be a guiding figure to follow and learn from.

That is what Deepak Chopra was, and is for me. The moment I woke up from conscious numbness a dear friend sent me a link with Deepak´s book, "The Way of the Wizard." Little did she know back then that I had just returned from an out-of-this-world moment of peace which changed my life forever. What a joyful co-incidence! I began listening to this audiobook immediately. That was July, 2016. His words were transforming my life, bringing light into every single cell, every little crevice in my soul. I was so thirsty, every page felt like a river in the desert I was coming out of.

In the month of August, my husband and I took an online seminar with Deepak and Eckhart Tolle: "Awakening to Higher Consciousness" where I learned I am not my perceptions or my thoughts and was able to see my life as a simple experience. That awareness changed my life again as it let me relax into the present, tasting Consciousness for the very first time. I continue to grow as I read and listen to Deepak´s teachings constantly.

So influential were his teachings to me that I found my purpose in life shortly after I finished listening to this audio book, which I had been delving in for more than 20 years.

Dear Deepak Chopra: you are a Guiding Angel, the father of my awakening process and I will always thank you and your team for your contributions to my life and to humanity.

Thankful

Vivian Baak

ACKNOWLEDGEMENTS

I thank Life, which for me has been a garden, a harmonious symphony, a walk in the Light. I've been guided day and night. Of course, the Source of All life always gave me good company and sent as angels along my path two wonderful human beings filled with love for me: my beloved parents, Edilma and Roberto. This is a way to pay them homage, to thank their many acts of love and their favors. All of my present joy is because I sprang from your roots and that of my grandparents. Thank you, mom and dad! Thank you grandma María Luisa and grandma Celina! Thank you grandpa Humberto and grandpa Herman! I know you watch me from above.

To my children. Joshua, my master in life; the greatest lessons of love I've learned from you and you know it. I am so fortunate to have you near. Hannah, you are the most beautiful flower that has graced my life. Thank you for choosing me as a mother. I love you both.

To my masters, those luminaries who have shared their knowledge with me.

Ernesto de León. How could I not call master he who hast taught me so much and managed to change the paradigms of my life; who has walked alongside with me on the long road that goes from the West to the East. Thank you, dear Master! I honor you and render unto you my devotion for your great contributions to my life.

To Benito Arriaga, who has devoted his entire life to studying sacred geometry and has managed to translate this knowledge for so many people like me. I am thankful for the treasures you have shared with me and applaud your work.

To Patricio Vega, who with love and sweetness has dared to teach me the postures which have allowed me to open up to life like a lotus flower, showing my beauty. With you I learned what is auspicious.

I express my gratitude to Luis Duarte, Chi Gong and Tai Chi professor, for the ease and authenticity with which you have led me flow with the Energy and let it move inside me, thereby greatly contributing to my integral sanity.

To all of those who have contributed to finalizing this book:
Raymond Aaron and Cara Witvoet, for their guidance and encouragement at each stage in the preparation of the book. Ana Paola Leiva, who unreservedly gave me her time in the revision of each chapter, thus showing me her unconditional love. I admire you, my strong and powerful friend. To Margarita Allen, poet, spiritualist, artist and angel of light, who was a key element in the book´s final stages. Eduardo Villagrán, a great writer and master, with whom I coincided for the English edition of the book and who reminds me that puzzle's pieces are perfect and attract each other, in the magnetic symphony that the whole of Humanity plays, making us what we are, which is One. To Mr. Guillermo Zúñiga, who reminded me

that whole purpose of all this is to help you, reader, heal.

To my friend Karla Payeras, who was the tool the Universe used to deliver into my hands the first book by the mentor of my awakening, Deepak Chopra, and the first person who saw the alchemy in me. To my friend Jennifer Kaltschmitt, who showed me her unconditional love by correcting my spelling errors and lending me support at each stage of my life. I love you, friends!

I have four wonderful brothers and sisters, whom I count among my greatest treasures: Regina (Chechi), the oldest, a great human being in a small container who is a key element in our family, with her jokes and wisecracks. Kareen is older than me, but that doesn't seem to stop her from following me in all of my adventures and awakenings. It is wonderful to have you as an accomplice, as I go through these changes and watch you blossom, heal and discover yourself as the divine being that you are. Devi, the youngest, but the greatest; I admire your strength, your tenacity and the way you have become the mainstay of our family. We are fortunate to have you with us. Roberto, for me Robertío. I still remember the day we found out you had been born and since that time completed our brood. Thank you for existing, I love you.

I thank friends that are like family, Patty Godoy, who has chosen to accept me and love me throughout all my radically different stages in life and beyond. Valerie Von Ahn who´s heart is always near to mine and one I cherish. Brenda Casado, I count you as one of my treasures, for we´ve cried, smiled and grown together.

Thank you Stormy Reynoso for being such a "Storm;" you were an alarm clock in my awakening process, I can still listen to your words trying to bring me out of my deepest dreams. Anayansi Serra I am so glad you organized those coaching seminars, thank you. I send you my love Fredy Benchoam (RIP) for seeing in me the jewels I hadn´t been able to notice.

This list has no end...

Thank you Life!

1. AWAKENING

A book on the joys of Self discovery

I was in the city of Antigua, Guatemala, sitting under an ancient tall tree. I was looking for inspiration and peace, in order to write a prospective vision of my upcoming years. I had just closed my business, which had left me feeling very tired; this involved packing all the stuff, finding safe storage for each of my belongings and letting go of a couple of employees that had worked for me for a long time. Now I was looking forward to rewriting my own story in order to get a clear idea of how to move forward.

Feeling tired and inwardly thirsty, I decided to take a couple of days of solitude in this beautiful city. The apartment where I was staying had beautiful gardens and was quiet enough. Just what I needed to relax and think!

The first day I went out to the garden with a notebook and pen, ready to write the venturous vision of what I wanted to do with my life.

Soon I realized that I had nothing to write. I felt so exhausted that my mind was blank, my creativity gone. I turned my head upwards and noticed the tree top that sheltered me from the sun: it was beautiful, verdant and imposing. This is the last I remember.

When I became aware of time again, I realized that over two hours had passed since the last time I had looked at my watch. I was sitting at the same spot, looking up the same tree. I didn't know if all that time I had been looking up, but my neck did not hurt. I felt flooded by a feeling of peace, rested and light, as though floating in clouds. The moment was so beautiful that I wanted to hold on to it, but didn't know how.

I looked at my cell phone and realized that a good friend had sent me a message, sharing the link of a book by Deepak Chopra, *The Way of the Wizard*, as well as a video dealing with some universal truths. I opened the link and listened to the recording. It seemed curious to me that I understood Deepak's words in such a familiar way, as when someone speaks to you in your mother's tongue. I felt at home after so many years of searching; the author's words were like a lullaby to me.

This hasn't happened to me again, but it changed my life as of that moment. Ever since, I became interested in the spiritual world and everything related to introspection and meditation. That event changed my inner thirst into curiosity about such subjects. It is said that the Master appears when the Student is ready.

This happened to me almost two years ago and just today another master happened to cross my path, to tell me that Buddha had a similar experience. I say similar without any intention of sounding arrogant, but of course Life surprised me once again when I read the link he sent me. I know little of Buddhism and have just started to read my first book on Tibetan philosophy!

Anyway, the link he sent me tells the story that after a long fast, Siddhartha Gautama sat under a sacred fig tree for several weeks, after which he experienced a state of complete awakening. Of course, my merits don't come close to those of the Buddha, nor have I come to a state of complete awakening, but what impressed me was that it happened to him under a tree! I received a gift from life which entircly changed my priorities and now I realize that great masters have also received great gifts under the auspices of a tree, which have changed their lives and the course of Humanity! What a co-incidence!

After that experience, I decided to take a sabbatical year in order to study the spiritual world. This has been my life's most important decision, the best that I could have taken at that time. My sabbatical year started in June 2016 and ended in July of the following year. I spent my days reading, watching videos, writing, meditating, quieting my mind and putting into practice what I learned each day. My progress was rapid; it seemed to me that those two hours under the tree made it easier for me to understand the spiritual world. I would receive messages all the time, which I would write down and continue to do so to this day.

This book, my web page and my Facebook page Find Peace and Heal are all the result of those two hours, a dream come true in what seems like a short time.
A few months after that experience, I resolved to teach some courses on Active Meditation, the name I give to the way in which I learned to meditate. Their main thrust was how to change our vibratory frequencies in order to find mental peace and thus enable a Western person to meditate in an easy and simple way. I invited some friends and relatives to take my courses and it was wonderful to be able to teach them what I practiced every day.

I knew this was my mission in life. After teaching my first class, in August 2016, I cried from the happiness of having found something that I had been after for a very long time. Finding my purpose is a gift from Life; I felt like a fish in the water, after believing for a long time that I was a monkey, trying to climb a tree!

Until then, I had been doing things that now seemed far away from my purpose in life. One cannot be happy in such a way; it's not common for a fish to find happiness in trees! However, I was an earnest fish. Among my personal achievements I graduated as a lawyer, though I never enjoyed practicing it. I worked as an interior decorator, as a garden designer; I had a kitchen appliance business, I had a restaurant, graduated as a fashion designer in Italy and the United States, worked as a volunteer for an international organization doing social work and finally I had a jewelry shop for 16 years! I also have two kids, 15 and 11, and have been married for 18 years.

Yes, I had been looking for a long time and all of a sudden "something" found me.

2. PEACE IS WITHIN YOU

a.   Yin Yang

In simple words, Yin Yan is an energetic center formed by feminine and masculine energy, where Yin is the feminine and Yang the masculine. This energetic center is always in motion because one type of energy attracts the other. This attraction is the infinite energy which expands the Universe. The synchronicity between feminine and masculine energies results in the process of creation, which is easier to visualize when one thinks of sexual relations; the feminine attracts, the masculine satisfies and the fruit of this synergy is the birth of a new life.

You have within yourself the potential to create anything and everything. This is why where there is a will, there is a way and you can accomplish anything you want. According to your purpose, so will be your propensity. Each person searches for what he or she likes, follows her propensities, which in turn illuminate her purpose in life. A painter likes to paint and a cook likes to cook; these are their purposes in life, what makes them feel good.

Perhaps at some point you have lost your inner peace because your husband or wife left you; or because you got fired from your job; or you don't know how you're going to pay your bills next month, and so on.

You say to yourself "I would feel better if only he hadn't left me; I could sleep better if I could pay my bills; I would be content if I had a job." Perhaps you haven't realized that the potential to make anything happen is within you. This may be compared to having a forgotten safe full of gold coins in your house, enough to pay for everything you need. You may have forgotten that within you is the wherewithal, all the information, all the power.

If you don't know about the huge potential you store in your heart, call it Yin Yang, you may wrongly believe that if your partner loves you and treats you right you will feel good and happy. Contrariwise, you may believe that if he or she leaves you, sadness and unrest will overwhelm you. In reality, what's happened is that he or she may have walked away with her own source of love, which she carries inside, but you have remained with your own source of love, which no one can take away from you! If you haven't learned to look inside yourself and to cultivate your own potential, I encourage you to do it.

The difference this will make in your life is nothing short of dramatic; it's like connecting, to an electricity source, the cables of a lamp that had never lit. The moment the lamp is connected light bursts forth; such is the purpose of the lamp. When you connect with your inner self, light will burst forth from you, inside out.

It is also important that you pay attention to your sexuality. If your physical being is blocked or damaged this will reflect itself on your spiritual being and you won't be able to liberate your creativity. All you see in the physical world is a reflection, a materialization of the spiritual world; you can see it with your eyes, but first you created it in your consciousness.

This is exactly what happens when a new life is conceived. Two people have sexual relations and, if a spermatozoid manages to penetrate an egg, a new material life will result, but its source is all that sexual energy that the woman and man set in motion. A new life is born and it is important to realize that it is the result of much the same type of energy which results in the creation of anything else, its materialization in the physical world.

Many people believe that creative sexual energy only pertains to intimate relations between man and woman. This shows an insufficient knowledge of the creative nature of energy in general. When you start a new project or a new business, it all starts with a wish, a desire to achieve something that you want to make true.

Next, you may experience a brainstorm. Then you examine your thoughts and give shape to your intentions; you put your ideas in order; your project takes shape. If such ideas persist and if you give them your time and attention, they will become a part of your everyday agenda.

Ideas result in meetings with teammates, suppliers, etc. Thus, the energy from these other persons will add up to your own, as a corollary to your original wishes and desires. Energy thus grows exponentially and thanks to this, projects are born; the time and efforts of all involved will sooner or later result in the materialization of a project in the physical world.

All that enthusiasm, effort and attention which is required to make a project come true shares the same essential energy as what is needed to conceive a child. It can be labeled sexual energy, or simply energy, because these two are essentially the same thing.

The essence of energy is to create, whether a new life, a project or a piece of work. Each new being, each new project and each new piece of work are the product of a subtle form of energy, which thanks to attention, dedication and care condense to the point of materializing in the world of the physical forms.

Whenever you think of energy remember that its intrinsic nature is to create, whether you wish to call it sexual or not. All energy yields new material expressions as a result; energy becomes matter.

One can also say that, just as each person has a soul, each project has a soul also; person and project are the condensation of an intention, of a bundle of creative energy. This is why I say that sexual relations can help explain the spiritual world; everything physical is a manifestation of Consciousness.

If you can understand that Yin Yang is within you, you will also realize that you are powerful and have the capacity to create anything and awaken all the love you need. Your feminine Yin aspect desires, attracts and inspires, whereas your Yang aspect fulfills your desires. For example, you may have wished to graduate from college when you were young. This wish, this desire, led you to register at a university, to study hard, to overcome any obstacle, until you held your diploma in your hands.

During your school years, when the many challenges overwhelmed you and tiredness set in, your concrete Yang energy would diminish, but your Yin energy, your feminine energy would come forth and remind you of your wish, your desire to finish school, thereby inspiring you to carry on. Can you see how these two forces work in synergy in order to enable you to create? Those school years gave you knowledge, made you grow, and turned you into a bigger person. This is what I call Expansion, which you achieve by putting your Yin and Yang forces into action.

Within you dwells all the potential; the potential for everything is in you. If you can assimilate this Universal truth, you won't lose your peace of mind with each and every loss. Even though you may feel pain and miss your beloved, you will have a reservoir of boundless love and abundance in your inner self, which will allow you to go on.

b.   Our Fortunate Nature

An old Indian tale tells the story of the god Brahma, who was alone and bored as the only conscious being in existence. He wanted somebody to play with and thus he decided to create a beautiful goddess named Maya, in order to have fun with her.

Once he created Maya, Brahma told her of his intention and she proposed to him to play a game, provided that he accepted all of her instructions. Eager to amuse himself, Brahma agreed. Maya instructed him to create the entire Universe, the Sun, the stars and the planets. She also told him to create life on Earth; animals, oceans, plants, the atmosphere, etc. Brahma followed Maya's instructions and created an illusion world.

Maya admired Brahma's creation and next told him to create an animal so conscious and intelligent so as to be able to appreciate his creation. Brahma created human beings and then asked Maya when their game would begin. Maya said: "right now", coming up close to Brahma and cutting him up into millions of small pieces and putting each piece inside a human being, exclaiming "let the game begin." She went on, "I will make you forget who you are, while you try to find yourself again. Only when you retrieve your unity and remember who you are will you have won the game; meanwhile, I will be winning." Till this day, the story goes, Brahma still struggles to remember who he really is and Maya keeps winning the game. Certainly, Brahma has had no time to be bored!

In other words, when you awaken from your dream and rediscover your divine nature you will become Brahma again and you will be able to assume your divinity, full of abundance and joy.

If you could see that Divinity lives within you, that you are part of a fractal of the Universe's greatest creative force and that in reality we all are one and the same because we are all fractals, then your reality will be radically different.

It astounds me how we feel and behave as though we were separate from each other; it's as though your little finger walked around by itself, proclaiming to the world to be an individual finger and struggling to find welfare and enlightenment, without realizing that, separated from the body, it's as good as dead, its capacities are non existing and its efforts useless. Could that little finger ever be happy?

However, we humans act in exactly the same way; we walk through life believing we are individuals, separated from the rest, disconnected from each other. Furthermore, we complain about being alone, in a human body composed of seven billion human beings! If that little finger awoke from its worldly illusion and saw itself walking around the streets, oozing blood and about to pass out, without blood or oxygen and unable to accomplish anything, for sure he would, if he could, run back and find its body, and reconnect to it immediately, with the hope of once again becoming part of a whole, coming back to life, feeling useful again, but especially to recover its state of calmness and get rid of the anguish in which it exists.

Your nature is divine and joyful. You are a divine being, able to create and expand, to heal yourself and others, but unfortunately often disconnected from them. If we are disconnected from our vital source, none of this is possible. We are nothing, if not connected to our source of Love, which in the story above is named Brahma, but you can name God; we are nothing and we can do nothing. This is the starting point, the first piece you have to put in place to return to your nature, full of joy.

The second thing to emphasize is that this Source of Life is within you and as such it is part of your essence. In 1964 a group of scientists, which included Peter Higgs, told the world about the Higgs Field. In order to test its existence, the LHC or Large Hadron Collider was built, a huge ring structure located in Geneva, Switzerland, which shoots particles so fast that when they collide with each other they disintegrate and leave traces, which allowed for observing the Higgs Boson.

This is a new particle, seen for the first time in 2012.

Mishiu Kaku explains that it lies at the origin of the Universe and all we see today. If all that exists was created in an explosion which became numberless parts, then all that exists is contained in that original particle and it remains present in all of its subsequent parts, which includes all of us. This is why it is also called sometimes "the particle of God."

Possibly, like many others, it is hard for you to accept that you are God because you were taught, as were we all, that God is a separate being, whose divine nature is opposed to yours, which is sinful. For many years, we believed that this superior energy was a different being, close to us as a parent to a child, but distinct.

Your entire life will change when you understand that God's particles are present in each of your cells; that you are made of Him or Her and therefore you are one and the same; and that this He or She is the vital flow that runs through your veins and gives you sustenance and support. You will understand the biblical verse that says "...the Church, which is its body, the plenitude of He who fills up everything." – Ephesians 1:23.

If you can understand what you are made of, it will be easier for you to be able to live in your divine nature of joy and peace.

c.   Beam the Light Inwards

Quantum physics has been of great help to be able to understand what happens in the material and spiritual worlds, which in reality are the same thing.

The experiment which gave birth to this branch of science was the "double slit" experiment. As Thomas Campbell explains, light is supposed to be a particle and if one makes it travel through a slit it should go in a straight line and make definite, discrete impacts. However, when light is made to travel through two slits, the pattern that forms on the other side is similar to water waves, although light is supposed to be matter and behave like matter; it is wavy and not linear, even if light particles are beamed one at a time!

So, they decided to install a particle detector to better observe light's behavior and they detected that each photon passed through one slit only and therefore the wave interference pattern was paradoxical. Scientists were confused as to the nature of light, whether it was formed of waves or particles, until Erwin Schrödinger postulated that light was neither, but instead a probability distribution, a wave function that would collapse as a particle upon observation, depending on how and where it is directed.

The following graphics will clear the idea of the double split experiments for you.

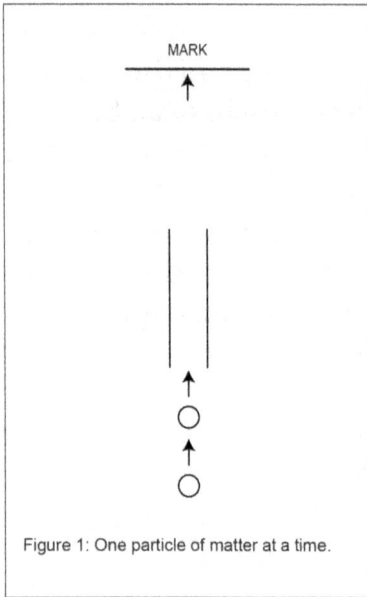

Figure 1: One particle of matter at a time.

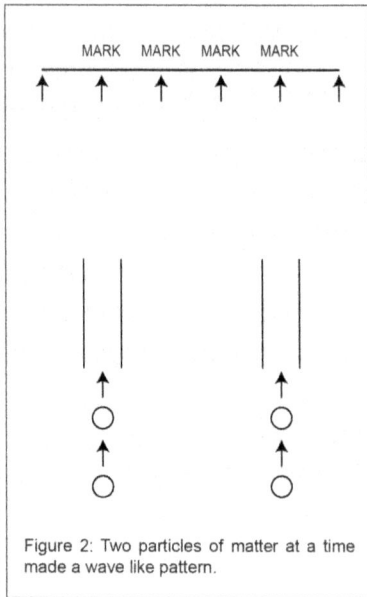

Figure 2: Two particles of matter at a time made a wave like pattern.

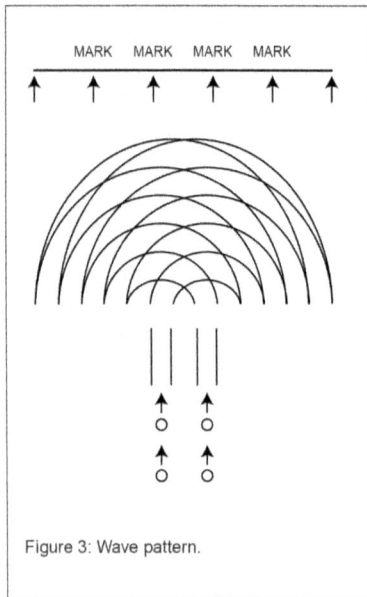

Figure 3: Wave pattern.

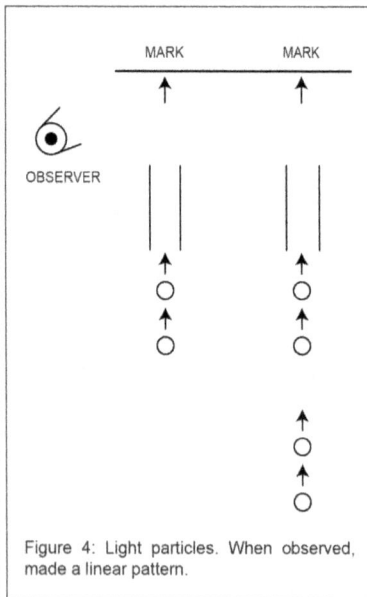

Figure 4: Light particles. When observed, made a linear pattern.

Thomas Campbell explained: "We seem to be talking about magic, but it isn't magic. It is just that while information is not observed yet, it does not really exist. It only exists as a probability. This sounds impossible because we live in cultures that exhibit an attachment to reality."

Nobel Prize winner Eugene Wigner said: "The very study of the external world led to the scientific conclusion that the content of consciousness is Universal reality." Albert Einstein said that "the physical space is a function of our conceptual regard," which means that our reality or what we believe as reality is directly related to our thought or what we think of it. Based on this, we can derive a very important Universal truth: Reality is a product of Consciousness.

The double slit experiment showed that, when observed, particles change their behavior, regardless of whether the observation was of past, present or future behavior. No matter where the observer is placed, the result is always the same.

I mention all this because at times past problems overwhelm you and rob you of your inner peace. You may believe that there is nothing you can do to change them and therefore you carry these memories with you during your whole life.

Understanding how particles behave under observation is a metaphor that shows that when you pay a certain type of attention to an incident which disturbs you or to a thought or memory from the past, it may cease to affect you in the same way and you may even redirect it.

In the past, I always thought that marriage was a load, an arrangement that would clip my wings and never understood how people could be married for a long time without feeling the weight of this load on their backs. I happen to be married to a partner who in no way subtracts from my life but on the contrary, contributes to it; a person who loves me and treats me right. Thus, I would not understand my feelings, but I would feel them anyway.

Through all my years in the Christian church and afterwards, during all of my coaching and self-improvement courses, I was not able to resolve these feelings of imprisonment and heaviness in relation to marriage. Of course, I wanted to clarify and understand these feelings, because I thought it was unfair to my partner and it made my path uphill without having any real fundaments.

When I commenced to look inside me, I was surprised. Wow! I had not beamed my light onto those spaces ever before.

Therein, I found many thoughts and ideas inherited from my parents, of course. My father was a very influential person in my life and always told me that marriage had clipped his wings. He not only said it but showed it through his actions.

My parents married very young, when they already had my older sister. Then they decided to get married when my mother got pregnant of my second sister. Perhaps what my father and mother wanted for their lives at that moment, was something else. He was 20 years old at the time and full of dreams. I can only imagine how he wanted to fly. They got married and obviously their lives greatly changed. My oldest sister suffered from scoliosis and they had another baby on the way. My parents were not wealthy and it must not have been easy for them to start a family from scratch. So, I understand and admire them; they are heroes for me, my sisters, my brother and my nephews and nieces.

Nevertheless, I had a conscious and unconscious message, saved in my brain, that marriage was a wing clipper. No wonder when my husband gave me an engagement ring I felt such contradictory emotions. It took me half an hour to answer, because I had to pray to find peace and with it an answer. He accepted me with all my caveats and confusion.

When I managed to look inside myself, the lamp of my consciousness shed light on this and other notions. The result was automatic; I no longer had to pray or invest additional energy analyzing the subject. It was enough for me to observe this notion to realize that it wasn't me, but just an idea, a thought, a memory, someone else's story, which didn't have to be mine.

This was sufficient for this notion to cease to affect me in the present and allowed me to align it with my wishes, such as observation does in the double-slit experiment.

There will be many things that the light of my inner observation will discover in the course of my evolutionary process and this fills me with anticipation and excitement. You have the capacity to redirect your life, your feelings, your emotions and the results of your actions wherever you want, today.

If you change your mind tomorrow, which is most probable, you can look inside again and change your destiny once more. This very knowledge will certainly bring you peace, as happened to me, and with it bring joy and fulfillment. It's a way to go back to your joyful nature and find your inner peace each day.

This inner observation has brought health to my marriage. Today I can say that, after a year and a half, I feel very light and happy. I have been married for 18 years and never thought I could say these words.

Thank you, life!

d. Find your Purpose in Life, Find the Joy of Peacefulness

How many times we've heard the question, what is your purpose in life? Anyone who has attended a self -improvement seminar or had some coaching has, like me, tormented his or her head with this question, the question of why we are in this world.

Most probably, your purpose in life was clearer when you were a kid. Perhaps you were a girl who liked to paint. Parents often see these proclivities as playful entertainments, which receive little attention compared to a child going to school. Maybe some parents can pay for painting classes as extracurricular activities that their child may enjoy, but still see them as simple hobbies, unrelated to the child's essence.

It may so happen that the girl goes to school and all she wants to do is painting: She paints her math notebook, her social sciences notebook, her agenda, the walls and the sidewalks.

As a consequence, she gets reprimanded by her teachers and her mother makes her wash the wall; she may even hide her crayons, unaware that the girl may be shouting inside "I am a great artist, who came to fill the world with colors!" But we adults are scared of the thought of a kid not finishing school, or college.

By that time, the adult woman will have forgotten why she came to the world. Perhaps she sees a beautiful painting and admires it, but from afar, something with which she no longer can identify. There are now too many layers between her inner self and the painting; everyday duties, things to do, things she should and shouldn't, her parents' expectations of her, the demands of marriage, household, kids, etc.

Later this woman wilts, loses her joy of life, ceases to shine and asks herself "Why am I here? Why did I come to this world?" She is like a fish which does not know its life belongs in the water and its purpose is to swim.

This is the story of my passion for art. When I was little, I had this notion clear in my head, but if a fish is forced to climb trees and a monkey to swim underwater things get a little difficult! It's nobody's fault; many off us are all confused in this sense. However, human beings are wonderful creatures. We assimilate change and have enormous learning capabilities, even though we may conform and accommodate for a while, in order to survive wherever we happen to be.

In my case, studying hard and getting good grades was a must. I got a lot of recognition and awards for my grades; the four women of my family turned out to be good students.

When I expressed my intentions to study art and design, my father agreed on the condition that upon my return from indulging in my hobby I would attend university and study a formal career. That's what I did. I went to Italy and the United States to study what I liked and because I liked it I succeeded. I earned scholarships and did not mind having to work all night on my design projects. I graduated with honors and, sadly for me at the time, the day came when I had to return to Guatemala. In my mind I was committed, but my heart beat to different tune. Nevertheless, a chip implanted in my head kept telling me I had to study a formal career.

I enrolled in law school, no less, while architecture was more to my liking. However, when I mentioned it to my father he said that I should not pick something which I had already studied elsewhere. Like a good daughter, I followed his guidance and got a law degree. I must confess that I had to work hard to retain all that stuff; I was like a fish trying to climb a palm tree!

As a lawyer, I only worked for my father and it felt to me like walking in the desert, especially going to the Commerce Registry, which for me was like a trip to the Sahara, with no oasis in sight. After five years I gathered up my courage and respectfully told my father that I would no longer write up his contracts; that I didn't like that profession and that it made me very unhappy.

My father was okay with this; he never opposed me when it mattered. I know he has always wanted me to be happy and always did what he thought was best for me. His advice for me to get a conventional degree was his best wish, at the time. I thank the Universe for all I learned during those years, which helped me become what I am now; but after all, I took a 12-year detour in my life, getting to know palm trees, when what I wanted was to explore the sea!

The point is, if you are a fish it may be difficult to find happiness on top of a palm tree! Life has many turns and I have been fortunate, thanks to some of those turns, to be able to touch bottom, as regards lack of inner peace. I did not get depressed, but I lost the connection to my vital energy, lost my shine. It's like a lamp that is disconnected; you feel you should be radiating light, which is in your nature, and instead you experience the uselessness of your existence. Perhaps you're doing things you were not designed to do!

It is important to reconnect with who you really are. Try to remember what you liked the most as a kid. That information is still present within you; maybe it's a small flame now, but it's still there.

Perhaps you don't know that a genius lives inside you. David R. Hawkins, in his book Power versus Strength, says the easiest way to understand the nature of a genius is to think of someone who is doing what he or she is best at doing, doing it in the best possible manner, according to his or her abilities.

Professor Hawkins relates a genius performance with the highest vibratory frequencies, which will be discussed later, and which calibration is similar to those of joy and peacefulness.

This means that if you manage to devote more time to doing what you love and makes you feel good and, even better, if you make it a source of income or just dedicate more time to it, you will be stimulating the genius within you. Hawkins also explains that this has nothing to do with your IQ, since this is a measure of your logical, academic and symbol recognition abilities, even though many geniuses do have high IQs. Hawkins says that genius is more related to innate abilities, which spring forth in response to personal likings and propensities and develop thanks to determination, dedication, courage, perseverance and passion.

I went back to painting three years ago. It was easy for me to take up brush and pencil again and handle them well. This reconnected me with my inner girl and became like a vital energy for me. The joy I felt each Saturday, going to my paint class and showing my professor my weekly progress, were food for my soul.

These were the first sparks that later helped me find the inner peace I was so ardently seeking. When I came home from each class, I was able to see everything in colors; my patience with my kids increased; I smiled during the weekends and slept happily at night.

This is the joyful nature I am talking about. Doing what you like and cultivating your innate talents, even when you're doing a job which doesn't seem to be your calling.

You can still connect with your inner child and little by little nourish the flame of that vital energy which is the source of your life. Peacefulness comes automatically when there is joy in the spirit.

This doesn't mean that you won't have to do things you don't like, such as doing accounting, paying your taxes, etc., but you will have the vital energy to do them to the best of your abilities. This is living connected to you joyful being, to your inner child, which will be food for your spirit and lead you to inner peace.

e. Back to Unity

Recall the story of Maya and Brahma. We have entirely forgotten what we are. We believe ourselves to be individual beings and struggle every day for our ideals, while we are indifferent to our brothers and sisters, to the rest of our body, which is all of Humanity.

Because of this individualistic mentality, we have become disconnected from Love. The Whole or the Divine Matrix is pure love. The source that nourishes us is love. Within this force, our existence makes sense; away from Unity we are nothing. We are just like that little finger I mentioned before, walking lonely and bloody, up and down the streets, away from its body. If we go back to love, aware that we are part of a collective Unity, a part of one whole thing, we will recover the sense of belonging that we so much miss.

We are fragmented in many ways. From the time we're born, we have been recording moments which have left their mark long after they have passed. Perhaps you heard your mother say: "she is so tall, thin and pretty" and you automatically recorded the message "women are pretty if they are tall and thin." Since we live in a world of opposites, we also recorded "short, plump women are not pretty."

With the passage of time, this memory has become petrified in your brain and to this day you think these thoughts, even though you may claim to believe otherwise. Thus, you have divided pretty and not-so-pretty women according to these characteristics. If you are fortunate enough to be tall and thin, you will feel separated from women in the other category. In this way, we have petrified in our minds millions of ideas that divide us from others; religions, social status, education, profession, civil status, etc.

All differences between us stem from ideas that have been programmed into our minds, calcifications from the past.

What is more important, we relate to each other based on these prejudices. If a well dressed adult approaches you, most probably you will greet him with respect, but if an ill-smelling beggar approaches you, your reaction will likely be to reach for a coin or walk away.

We are not relating to the person we have in front, but rather to the judgment we already have of such a person, something we have ourselves made up, based on our past impressions.

The differences we perceive between us are comparisons from our past impressions, but not part of our essence. When a sculptor does not like the result of his work, he can remake the piece as many times he likes. The essence of the sculpture is always the same clay, even though one time he creates a woman, next time an abstract piece and next a ship.

The essence of the sculpture is clay. What your eyes see is the shape of a woman, an abstraction or a ship, all dissimilar and perhaps some more beautiful than others, but if we analyze their essence they are not so different from one another; they are different expressions of clay's possibilities, different manifestations of the same clay.

Your physical body, furthermore, is not all that you are; you are only experiencing a body. The same is true in relation to the mind; you only experience thoughts and memories.

A teacher once explained to me that the mind is like a cell phone with a memory that is overcharged to the point of saturation; likewise, our minds overcharge with inputs and we lose connection to our inner self. We confuse our being with our thoughts because this is what we have been taught, but in reality we are much bigger than that.

Our thoughts are limited by our circumstances, our culture and our knowledge; what we really are is greater than these limitations imposed by the material world. In reality, you are Conscience experiencing body and mind. Since we never turn off the mind, however, just as we seldom turn off our cell phones, we have come to believe that we are our thoughts, when we are really much more. We are pure Love, pure consciousness.

If you manage to relate to life from the standpoint of Unity, not emphasizing differences, you will return to the fountain of love you so much crave. You will never feel alone; you will feel the contentment and satisfaction of a sense of belonging.

A practical way to find out whether you are relating to life from the perspective of Unity and not from the standpoint of petrified ideas is whether you are able to enjoy each person, each moment and each place without labels or judgment. For example, if you walk into a place and you say to yourself "this is similar to such and such a place" or "this reminds me of..." or even "this doesn't look so clean"; or if you are introduced to a person and immediately your mind looks for the likenesses to somebody else and you label her good, bad, pretty, ugly, friendly, arrogant, etc. on that basis; then you are relating to life from the standpoint of perceived differences.

The opposite would be to get to know a new place, a new person or even an old one and be able to enjoy the experience without resorting to labels, accepting it for what it is and enjoying it in full consciousness and love.

Because of our judgments, labels and opinions, we have created much suffering in the world. We have limited our capacity to enjoy people, things and places in a light-hearted manner. Judging and labeling everything requires a lot of energy and it ends up draining us.

To connect with life again means to relate to life from the standpoint of Unity, while suffering is relating to life from the standpoint of judgment. We all wish to heal our lives; we need to find inner peace.
To do this we have to stop judging and labeling each and all things.

We even judge our own bodies and may have a label for each of its parts; the long nose, the bulging tummy, the bandy legs, the dry hair, etc. Thus, we are divided within ourselves. We don't fully accept our bodies for what they are and are not able to feel, enjoy and simply experience them. The abundant happiness we find when we accept ourselves and others, places and circumstances, our own lives, is a return to the unity of life and love. As a result we find peace and therefore we heal ourselves.

The purpose of Life is the return to Unity.

f. Unity to Change the World

What will we say when Brahma becomes one again? Will the game be over? Or will we say that Brahma finally recognized himself and will never be the same again? I think that what is true for us is true for Brahma as well. When we stop perceiving ourselves as individuals and understand that we are part of a Whole, we stop judging ourselves and others and many things will change.

Perhaps you'll have the same experience I had. When you understand yourself to be part of a fractal Whole, you will experience pure power. You will feel capable of anything, one with the source of all information and full of vital force. Like the Prodigal Son, you will come home from scarcity, impotence, loneliness and anguish. Security, joy and peace come when you recognize yourself as a piece of the fractal of Totality.

We often say that help comes from "up there", referring to the sky or to heaven. You have to realize that you don't have influences up there, but that you are "up there"; up there is within you. Deepak Chopra states it in his book The Way of the Wizard, "You are the center of the Universe." Now you can understand it, experience it and give thanks for your divine nature. Observing the great amount of judgments, opinions and labels that I had for every person and everything was a shock for me. I had heard the injunction "do not judge" many times and believed that it was not right to criticize others, but to understand that labeling separates me from the essence of others and the essence of things, and therefore from the source of all things, which is God, is a piece of information that I am still processing.

Many ideas and memories of the past keep dissolving as I engage in their observation.

I continue to label, qualify and judge, but I also realize that I am evolving towards Unity and acceptance, enjoying the present and people in the here and now. I believe this process is also part of the source, a part of God as I continue practicing introspection and reconnecting with my inner self in search for purity and sanity.

I feel very thankful for the guidance I have received till now, which allows me to light up my inner being. It is exciting for me to witness the expansion of my own self, which is also the expansion of Humanity's consciousness and this fills me with hope.

Last, returning to the Unity, I can tell you that it requires humility. Benito Arriaga, a master of Sacred Geometry, explains that we are used to believing only what we can test and see. What the mind approves of we consider valid. It is arrogance, on our part, to try to rationalize everything. Thus, we need humility to accept that there are things which we cannot see and yet exist.

You need to understand that what your mind can perceive is a limited part of the Whole. You cannot see Peace, yet you can feel it and its absence results in anguish. We even fight each other over our viewpoints, when they are so limited and invisible. Dethroning matter requires humility, which brings me back to unity with the Whole.

We will change the world from the standpoint of unity; not from individualism, but from the perspective that we are the Whole, all of us united as of one body. We will become One when we cease labeling, judging and forming opinions about everybody and everything; when we understand that without labels we can experience everything as well as each other; enjoying ourselves without investing energy in the differences we see, but rather living in the unity that we are.

This will only happen when in all humility, we dethrone matter and reason, accepting there are things that we don't see and yet exist; that there is much we don't understand and yet is valid. Walking together towards the expansion of Consciousness, we will change the world!

Our planet is in continuous evolution and so are we. We change together in synergy. How far can we go if we act in Unity and as One?

g. Maintaining your Energy Source

Just as a car needs gas to move, plus maintenance and service to function adequately, you need to constantly reconnect with the source of vital energy or Divine Matrix or God.

No doubt you want everything to work out right for you: at work, in your relationships, you want a wholesome body and you wish to not prematurely age. But are you doing enough to achieve all of these things?

If you are reading this book, you're surely thirsty for change; or perhaps your awakening process has already started. Little by little, you will be able to see things more clearly, including the need for the continuous maintenance of your body and spirit. The vibration you experience at each moment in your life will attract more people and things, vibrating with the same frequency. For example, following my personal awakening, the right information happened to come my way.

First, a book recommended to me by a dear friend, who has remained close to me during my awakening. It is Deepak Chopra's The Way of the Wizard. The second source of information was contained in countless YouTube videos dealing with the internal and external worlds.

These to me were like fresh rivers on the driest land. I craved for more; I watched those videos 17 times, learned them by heart. The Way of the Wizard became my constant companion.
I listened to its audio version another 17 times! I went on to other related sources and met people involved with our return to Unity and our reconnecting with the Universe.

Many things happened; or I attracted them. One time I was talking to my orthodontist, no less, and he went on to explain the origin of civilizations and how Humanity lost connection with the Universe. That very day he sent me and continues to send very interesting videos on the subject. Surely before that I was vibrating in such a way as to not attract this kind of relevant information.

Ever since, not a day passes when I don't read, listen to or receive a class related to these subjects. For instance, I took a 40 day course on how to reconnect with the heart of Humanity, sponsored by an autistic master, Daniel and his intermediary Deborah O. Baker. They were of great help for me and taught me how to enter the center of my being and connect with the Universe in an easy and practical way; I call it active meditation.

Further on I attended an event held by Anna Saranande, who was visiting Guatemala and who taught me to connect with Mother Earth. This closed a loop for me. I learned how to form the circuit that kept my inner light on: Divine Matrix, Mother Earth and I as the transmitter.

Negative and positive energies come from the Universe and Earth, Yang and Yin; it is a constant flow of vital energy which provides us with nourishment. My inner light turned on again and I went back to the joy of my nature and abundant peace.

As part of my evolutionary process, I practice Qi Gong, which is a type of exercise based on Chinese Medicine techniques that combines breathing, physical exercises and mental power to improve health, heal pain, eliminate stress, anxiety and depression and increase and improve the flow of energy and vitality. This practice cleanses the body and the spirit, taking energy and oxygen not only to our organs but also to every cell of our body; it allows us to flow with the Universe and Earth without obstructions.

I have had the opportunity to participate in two Tantra Yoga retreats, where I met Carol Schneider, a brave and humble fighter of a woman, who has a lot to teach on subjects such as mental health, the workings of the human ego and the return to Unity. I thank God for these two retreats. Attending them changed my life.

The Tantra Yoga postures, which I continue to practice, also help me find the sacred spaces within myself, stimulate the sacred intuition which I had lost. I meditate in order to stir my body's vital energy, awaken and heal chakras, or vital energy centers located along my back, which act as energy receiving portals stemming from the Universe and Earth and which have repercussions on my Subconscious and on my emotions.

Tantric practices are effective tools to reconnect with your energies and yields positive results very quickly, both in your body and your mind; I thank my teachers Patricio Vega and Carol Schneider for sharing their love, knowledge and wisdom with me.

Now I write every day; it has become my priority. Sharing with others my awakening and helping them along their evolutionary path has become my purpose in life. Finding this purpose was a great gift for me; I immediately prepared some courses which my friends and family attended and when they were over I knew that henceforth I would spend my time preparing myself, studying and concentrating my energies in doing this job as well as I possibly can.

Healing and reconnecting with the Matrix involves mind and body. Therefore, I also study Chinese Medicine, ancestral knowledge which teaches us that illness is the result of a disconnection between the body and the nature and Cosmos.

This applies to mental illnesses as well. Chinese Medicine is gaining ground in the Western world as well, thanks to its positive results.

It has withstood the test of time and has no side effects; it goes hand in hand with the laws of nature and the Qi, or vital energy.

I have also started to grow my own vegetables and herbs and this has taught me the intrinsic value of relating to the Earth directly, with gratitude and admiration. The Earth, in return, has given me what I need, both as nourishment and as remedy. All the food and water we take in, as well as the oxygen we breathe, can be considered cleansing and healing agents for our body and soul. If you reconnect with them, you will also heal.

For the time being, I want to encourage you to start somewhere; whatever calls your attention, be it taking care of your body or of your spirit, but start your healing process right away. One thing will lead you to another.

You are a divine being with capacities not even you can fathom at this time. If you profit from the treasure you have in your own body and mind during your lifetime, you will see "things that no eye ever saw, nor any ear heard" – Corinthians 2:9.

Start doing what you like. Follow your natural propensities. This is the easiest way to reconnect with your inner child and your vital energy. Yoga, Chi Kung, meditation, Ayurveda Medicine, Chinese Medicine, cultivating your cosmic vision, practicing a diet that is less and less toxic, retreats; these are some of the paths that I have followed and which have helped me and therefore can help you to awaken, reconnect with your inner being, heal and return to your joyful nature. There are many ways to do it and we have a lot to learn. Fortunately, today we can make use of a lot of information, available at our fingertips.

This chapter has developed the subject of peace within yourself, so that later you may understand that your exterior and physical health is also within you, from the perspective of unity I have herein proposed. Now I would like to show you another angle of this same Unity, which is Acceptance.

The moment you manage to accept yourself and your circumstances, the country where you live, the World and the planet that we all share and stop fighting with yourself and others, you will find sanity in your life and you will return to the unity of peace and abundance I have been talking about. The joy of life is ultimately based on Acceptance.

3. PEACE AND ACCEPTANCE

a. Acceptance

Tantra refers to that which expands wisdom in life. She who is tantric is a lover of life. Tantra teaches that permanent enlightenment, or liberation, can be achieved while one remains in the physical state and for that it makes use of techniques that awaken consciousness in the course of everyday life; this results in emotional unblocking and freeing karmic patterns. (enbuenasmanos.com). Tantra invites you to accept all the colors and flavors that life has to offer. Hard to believe as it may be, every situation, every moment and every day are enjoyable.

The bad taste in your mouth stemming from an amorous breakup is enjoyable, even if you loved the person. If you are going through something of the sort it may be difficult for you to understand what I am saying; but it may be that a breakup may prod you into looking inside yourself for that which always seems to lead you to such situations and this in turn may lead to some answers and this is enjoyable.

Closing a business may seem like a painful failure to many, but in my case it led me to close one door just to open another. Now I am devoted to cultivating my inner Self and have awakened to my joyful divine nature. I would not go back to my former situation, where I felt trapped by the particulars of my business and far from peaceful.

My nephew had a cardiovascular accident; his brain central artery burst and he almost died. It took months for him to recover; he had to learn to speak and walk again. Everyone felt that a great mishap had fallen upon him. However, it turned out to be like a trigger that helped Erick find his passion in life and turned his life around. He used to work as an internal auditor for a soft drink company and now he is a dog trainer! He owns a pet hotel and day care center and wrote a book – *A Tail of Miracles* -; he also shares motivational talks and has become a public figure in Guatemala and beyond. He has found his passion in life.

Life is just a moment, my father says. And I add "and each moment has a different flavor." No matter if a flavor is bitter, bland or sweet; all of Life's flavors eventually pass. None is intrinsically good or bad; you are just used to some more than others and change is always challenging.
For example, we may be so used to sugar that its absence makes us feel that something is missing. The same thing happens with the moments we are used to calling disagreeable.

My oldest sister often says that when she is going through some big problem, it feels like she's dying but she never does. She is the funniest of the bunch and always says this with a smile. When you accept the disagreeable moment, person or situation, the bad taste in your mouth loses its strength and becomes tolerable. Before we know it, it has dissolved itself in all the other flavors and colors of Life, in its Unity.

Most of our suffering is attributable to our mind's ideas and perceptions. When we actually live through a situation, we realize that it wasn't as bad as we feared it would be. It's like being afraid of darkness and turning on a lamp: you realize that there were no grounds for your fear. Observation and acceptance make our negative thoughts fade away.

b. Ho'Oponopono

My chiropractor introduced me to the ancient Hawaiian prayer that changed my perspective about the concept of Unity.

Dr. Torres-Fry's clinic has a mystical aura, in part due to the fact that he always burns incense. One time I went to see him for back pain treatment and I noticed a sign that said *I am sorry, forgive me, I love you, Thank you.* When he saw me reading it, he calmly said "ho'oponopono." He went on to explain that it was an ancient Hawaiian prayer and that whenever he was driving in traffic he would repeat these words, in order to send positive vibrations instead of the usual complaints.

He was, however, telling me something else, which my inner self perceived. When I got home I found a book on the subject and devoured it; it was like an ointment on my wounds. Ho'oponopono is based on the notion that, granted that we are all One, whatever each person does is also done by everybody else; we are all responsible for everything and everyone.

Think of someone who has committed murder. What would the jury think, if in his defense the murderer would argue that it wasn't him who did it, but his hand? He would claim that it is his hand which has to go to jail! In our material world, we judge the hand, send it to prison and pretend that it will reform to the point it will be able to rejoin society, when in the end we are all responsible!

I felt like I had discovered a hidden treasure and that is exactly what I found. I took up the Hawaiian prayer and often repeated "I am sorry, forgive me, I love you, thank you." This phrase has a very high vibratory frequency, both healing and compassionate. Divinity is approached when we understand that we are One and that we can apologize to anyone, even to a criminal, because I also suffer for his crimes which are also mine. When we apologize we acknowledge the weight we all carry, the guilt and remorse for hurting others and thus we free ourselves from these misplaced feelings.

I may even ask for forgiveness from a person whose evolutionary process I or my ancestors have curtailed, consciously or unconsciously; forgiveness for having acted without regard for the divine laws of harmony and love. When we judge somebody or a situation we are ignoring our spiritual connection to the Whole. (*Ho'oponopono*, by Ulrich E. Duprée).

I can tell a murderer that I love him as much as I love myself because we are One. I can see his divinity and accept his situation from a loving perspective. I can love the problems that have opened my eyes and allowed me to realize our physical constraints. I can love the person unconditionally, with all of his or her defects and faults, which are also mine.

Last, I can thank a person because awareness of our unity makes me realize that a miracle has begun to take place. I can thank God and the Angels because I know they are working on my behalf. I can also thank anything that happens because I understand the laws of cause and effect. And I can be grateful because the power of forgiveness has set me free from the chains of the past, from all those negative energies, as in our collective consciousness, our unity, the murderer may also be set free. (Adapted from *Ho'oponopono*).

This prayer and my awareness of Unity have helped me rescue my relationship with my 14 year old teenage son. I always knew this stage would be a challenge for us, in part because of his temper. He is a smart, charismatic and competitive boy, with a spark of natural presence, who likes to stand out and doesn't stop until he gets what he wants. At his young age, he would like to eat the whole world in one bite! He goes through life faster than his circumstances allow, not mentioning his mother, if she had a choice. In the most difficult and challenging moments, when I see him wanting to taste and challenge everything in such a reckless fashion, the Ho'oponopono prayer has reminded me of our unity and my capacity to share his life's thrashings, wherever I happen to stand in relation to them.

At one point, my son developed a very disdainful attitude towards his father, increasingly loveless and thankless. They stopped talking to each other when his father got tired of begging for his affection. One day, Joshua and I happened to be alone and I asked him what is his problem, why was he so mean-spirited to his father, when Cristian has always been a very present, caring father. He had a hard time coming out with it, but finally said that he didn't like his father and had no patience with him. After he said this he got out of the car and I cried and felt a lot of pain, because Cristian has been so good to all of us.

Some days went by and I continued saying the Ho'oponopono prayer on behalf of my son. One night during dinner, while he was at the table acting as though he was doing us a big favor just by being there, I felt the pain again when he gave a very brusque answer to his father's hello. I stood up and walked to the kitchen and at that moment I received what seem to me to be a message from the Matrix, the web that connects us to our divinity, our inner Self. It said: "You have acted equally brusque, indifferent and ungrateful towards Cristian many times and now you are seeing it expressed in your son." I almost dropped the dish I was carrying, turned around and looked at them and Ho'oponopono came to my mind.

From that moment on, I was the one who changed. Ho'oponopono allowed me to realize that it was I who was vibrating with a negative frequency, such that it had materialized in my own son, in the form of negative attitudes towards my husband. Then I understood the saying that all change begins within you and if you wish to change the world, first change yourself.

Ever since, I have felt an almost delicious need to show my husband affection and gratitude. In the past, I was blinded by my own shortcomings and individuality. Now that I can see, my sanity has patently increased; it manifests itself in a feeling of abundance, peacefulness and indescribable joy.

The magic of Ho'oponopono comes from accepting that all change I wish to see in the world begins with me; it provides a direct route to our complete sanity, in a context of peace. You can go to my web page **www.findpeaceandheal.com**, and find a free of charge, guided meditation for you to follow through. This is a gift I want to share with you to help you heal your relationships and thus heal yourself as well.

c. The Root Chakra

Energy is to our consciousness as fuel is to a car. We need energy and vitality in order to function. Your consciousness, your soul, your spirit and your body make up your whole being and all of them need a supply of vital energy. Perhaps you thought that only your body needed nourishment, but your spirit needs it too; in some instances, in a literal sense as well.

Chakras are the vertices or connectors, receptors of energy emanating from the Universe towards Earth. Through them, your body can receive these energies. Your being receives energetic nourishment through the chakras within you, which although not necessarily physical, regulate your body and your emotional being.

Your body's main chakras are seven; two of them are at the base of your spine and are closely related to our capacity for acceptance. If our lower chakras are damaged, life stops flowing; they become life's locks instead of its portals.

The root chakra is Muladhara. Discussing it at length would fall outside the scope of the present book, so I will just talk about it in relations to peacefulness and sanity. This chakra regulates one's self confidence, the survival instinct, and our relationship to money; the feeling of belonging and trust; where you stand and how you connect to the Earth, your physical reality.

Upon looking closely, all of these have to do with Acceptance. If you can't accept yourself, you won't have confidence in yourself, much less in others. If you can't accept your role in life, as daughter, as wife, as brother or as a professional, you will have a lot of impediments to feeling well and at peace. You have to accept your reality if you want to move forward in life and the key word is Acceptance.

As for me, I can say that I used to always fight with the country where I live. Although Guatemala is a beautiful country and has treated me well, I was not happy living there. One of my dreams has been to live in another country and it's still on my bucket list.

While I worked to reconnect with my inner Self and to Unity, I had a sense of frustration for not being able to leave the country and unconsciously blamed my husband for it. My mind kept telling me that he didn't dare to leave and that forced us to stay in Guatemala. Months went by while I lived with this and devoted myself to introspection and to finding my peace.

Cristian's mother is an older woman, who lives with us at home. She has been increasingly losing her mind's and her body's faculties. She suffers from senile dementia and is increasingly becoming like a baby. Nevertheless, when I thought of leaving, I did not worry about her; I knew we would find an adequate solution for Tony, so that didn't stop me from dreaming of going away.

The solution was unexpected and not short of miraculous. One day I stopped feeling the urge to leave Guatemala; I felt at peace in this country. My mother-in-law's face came to my mind; I saw her sitting in her chair, as she spends most of her days and I smiled, realizing that this is the role that I have to perform at the present time. I suddenly knew that I would leave Guatemala when Tony no longer needed us; I also know that she has still many years to live. This country has been good to me because it is the place where I have to be at this time. What a wonderful feeling!

The Matrix and Mother Earth have been taking care of me and in turn I do my best to take care of my husband, my children and my in-laws; it's like a cascade of love. Since we brought Tony to live with us, we moved to a bigger house. I am a lover of plants and animals and in this house I have place for more of them.

When I knew we were moving to this house I started looking for a dog and found a couple of beautiful Weimaraners. I am so happy! These dogs have been through rough times, whereas at the house we love them and in return they guard our house with fidelity.

Then my sisteres knew we had more space, so they gave us a macaw that used to live with us at home when we were kids. This macaw is now our favorite pet and lives freely at the house, decorating our garden with its colorful plumage.

Now we also have a cute and affectionate parrot. It amuses the hell out of us with its pranks. Last, at this house all of my orchids blossomed, which they didn't at our previous apartment. Bottom line, moving to a larger house to accommodate my mother in law turned out to be a greater gift for me and while our expenses grew so did our income.

My father in law is now living with us as well. He comes from a small town far away from the city with no doctors while he increasingly requires medical attention. We are enjoying his presence, his war stories and his tales as a ship captain. We all laugh together when he loses his teeth or misses his turn at cards. Of course, we have been spending more time and energy, but I knew this would be the case and as a matter of fact with his arrival our lives grew in every sense.

Perhaps I don't have as much time for social events or to do shopping, but I am incredibly happy! I tell you all these things to share with you how much my life changed once I accepted the fact that this is the place I should be at this time and made peace with the notion of staying here.

Another important element of the root chakra is being able to accept that, wherever you are, your mission is always to make your contribution not only to the country but also to your family and to all the people and places around you. You are there to give love and foster the improvement of those people and places, while you yourself continue to evolve as well. We are all part of a Unity and to the extent that you make your life better everything around you will also improve, as will the world.

One of the reasons why the root chakra may be impaired is that many of us in the Americas retain the spirit of the "Conquistadores", which asks "what can I get out of this place?" instead of asking ourselves what we can contribute to our place of residence. My chakra teacher Benito Arriaga explained this to me. As the saying goes, "If you are no good to others, you are no good." Healing yourself requires a change in mentality, from taking to giving. This applies at work, to your family, to your marriage, to your country and to the world.

It's called root chakra because it is like the root of a tree, indispensable to its life. Roots nourish trees. Can you think of a tree that is disconnected from the earth, a tree that rejects its roots? How can you heal yourself and find peace if you are not connected to your family, your country and the world? The state of being disconnected is similar to the state of being dead.

One way to find out whether you are disconnected from your roots is whether you have feelings of bitterness. The way to healing is to reconnect with your roots, at this place and at this time in your life. Sanity and vitality will return when you accept your place in the here and now. Like anything else, you are connected to the Whole via your roots, which give you the means to receive whatever you need to grow and help others. I am talking about the synergy each cell has with the tree. Each cell has the right to receive oxygen and nourishment needed to multiply, so that the tree can grow and give fruit.

Another way to find out whether your root chakra is impaired is to ascertain whether you feel secure and comfortable with yourself, your marriage, your country and your work. When your root chakra is impaired, you may experience pain or problems in your bones, which like the roots of a tree, provide you with support.

Even though you may not like everything about your life right now, accepting it is the first step to make it better. When I dislike my country, my marriage and my family I am rejecting my own vitality because I automatically contract my muscles in a reflex of resistance and this obstructs the flow of vitality through my body. It's like when you bend a water hose and interfere with the flow of water. When you do this to yourself you develop obstructions that block your body from expelling toxins and waste and as a result these stay inside you and your spirit withers.

Your discomfort may come from being unable to accept yourself, the person that you see in front of you, but if you accept this person without resistance the moment will pass without consequences. Resistance is our next subject.

d. Stop Trying to Control Everything

I wish to control my kids, have them be the way of my dreams and behave as I wish, but in most cases the exact opposite happens. Since they turned out different than I expected, maternity was a shock to me, and a source of unease.
My first kid was planned, desired and wished for. I prayed a lot for his wellbeing and tried to visualize him as a perfect child, in accordance to my preconceived notions. I could not have been more wrong!

When this child was born, and even in the womb, he showed me his essence in an unmistakable way, but I refused to see it. How could I, when I was praying and trying to visualize a perfect child "my way" every day. During one of the ultrasounds he kept moving so much that, at my suggestion, Cristian tried talking to him and it worked! We only have one picture of his little face during my whole pregnancy.

When the nine months passed I was expecting my perfect child to be born on December 26, as per the doctor's forecast, but the days passed and my nervousness increased. This was not as planned in my agenda or in my prayers. Why wouldn't he come out?

My preconceived ideas did not come true and showed me how wrong I was, in trying to control everything. How arrogant of me to even try to control two human beings who happen to be my kids! As a mother, I fell flat upon my face. My ideas about light blue pajamas smelling of lavender talcum were blown away by my kid's temper. He would not sleep, he would hit every person that approached him and he destroyed his toys; he only smelled of talcum the second he came out of his bath.

To this day, my child continues to teach me the most beautiful lesson of unconditional love, which makes us parents accept our children's decisions, even though they may seem wrong to us and accept their temperaments even though they may irritate us through their attitudes and sometimes their indifference, which certainly may hurt. But at the magical moment when we accept them as they are we ceased to resist. When you let go of the hose you bent, the water again flows freely and with good pressure.

The same is true about the love for our kids; when we stop resisting them and accept them as they are, our love flows to them and we become capable of accompanying them on their path, hug them when they get hurt as a consequence of their own decisions, watch them blossom in life, shine with their own light and find themselves as well, discovering who they are and why they are in this world. This is why I deeply thank my son Joshua, one of the persons who has taught me the most about love up until now. A treasure in my life!

A friend of mine shared an experience she had while at the beach in Spain sometime ago. She went into the ocean and was hit by a wave that made her lose her footing and took her bathing suit away. Being under water, she feared for her life, as her body experienced a nervous shock.

Suddenly she had the idea of letting herself be carried away by the wave without resistance and relaxed her body, even when she went underwater, until she finally resurfaced and was able to breathe. She let herself be carried away until the sea itself returned her to the beach, naked and far from the spot where she went in. She was going through a difficult period at the time and took this experience as a lesson.

While this is a lovely metaphor, I do not necessarily recommend it as a life-saving technique, when an ocean wave carries you away!

When you resist life's difficult situations, you tense up and things get worse; the shocks from the waves feel stronger because you are like an inflexible rock. Besides, you become heavier and it becomes harder to float back to the surface. But when you stop resisting you automatically relax your body and your soul. You stop fighting the wave. When you are full of fear and resistance it is difficult to see things clearly and you lose your common sense, but when you practice acceptance you automatically relax.

Resistance to situations may be compared to a tree standing in the way of a speeding car. If the tree is flexible, the car might pass over it with little damage, but if the tree is rigid the consequences may be severe. Why does one wishes to control everything? In my case, I was afraid that my son would hurt himself because of his own restlessness; or that he would seriously hurt another child; I was even afraid that he could drown in his own saliva during the night! Can you recognize the key word in all of the above? The key word is fear. Even to this day, I sometimes fear for him; his life on the fast lane, his penchant for danger, his intensity and recklessness. His favorite sport is racing cars! This is an important part of his essence and always has been. It's natural for mothers to fear for their children but again, my son has taught me that through acceptance I can find peace as a mother and be able to see the healthy side of our relationship as mother and son.

I am learning to let my children make mistakes, now that they are young; hurt themselves, miss a year at school, misplace their clothes and so on. In terms of energy, time and money, their mistakes are less costly now. They themselves will become able to see the consequences of their own actions; when their friends progress in school and they don't, when they no longer have good sweaters to wear, they might become more studious and more careful. Experience is the best teacher.

Fear is a preconceived idea. It stems from your memories or those of your forbearers. Your mother might have instilled in you the fear of getting sick from not wearing a sweater, while it took me years to discover that not wearing a sweater does not necessarily leads to getting a cold.

Fear is nothing but your ego, telling you that you are about to lose control of a situation. Your ego knows that the moment you let yourself be carried away by the wave, it will dissolve in the wide sea and you will be rid of it.

As you practice letting go, acceptance or flowing with the wave, letting time and distance do their work, letting your children make mistakes, miss a school year, anything that does not seriously threaten their safety and security, your connection with your inner Self will become stronger, as well as your peacefulness and sanity. The flow of life will be able to pass through you or carry you on without obstructions or undue resistance caused by fear.

When you are afraid, your breathing accelerates and shortens, your heart beats faster and you can't think clearly; instead when you are at peace you breathe more deeply and your ideas flow more easily.

Fear can deplete your vital energy; it discharges your battery, so to speak, by keeping you in a permanent state of resistance, tense and consuming lots of energy.

Contrariwise, a state of peace and relaxation allows your body to recover its vital energy. It is important that you stop relating to life from the standpoint of fear and worry and that you seek moments of peace and relaxation in your everyday life.

Accept yourself and those nearest to you; seek the roots of your tree until you fully accept the place where you live, your relatives, your friends, and your job, and so on till you reach a state of acceptance of the world in which we live. Acceptance will lead you to inner peace and peace will help you achieve complete healthfulness in your life.

c. Enjoy Life

This means accepting this very moment in your life. Even though you have not reached all of your goals, or if you don't like your job or your income, even though you dislike your past or the results you have so far obtained, your reputation, what you have destroyed and what you haven't started, what you left unfinished, you can accept and embrace your life with love if you learn to enjoy this very moment.

Why do you always want what you don't have? Why do you focus on what you have not achieved instead of enjoying what you have? Why do you want your son or daughter to behave differently? Why do you want to have a different look? When I ask of you these questions, I am also asking myself, believe me. I don't have access to absolute truth and precisely because I am in the process of searching, I can share what I have so far managed to perceive.

All of these questions have one thing in common: inconformity. Again, your inconformity is a result of your disconnection with the Matrix, the source I have been talking about. I can say this not from access to absolute truth, but as a serious participant in the process of finding it.

Many times it is impossible for you to accept someone or something because of the standards that society has imposed on you. For example, you may be convinced that your body must have a certain size and shape, or that your marriage has to last forever, or that you must have children to become a complete person.

The same goes for cars, your house, nice clothes, voyages, furniture, sizable bank accounts, as measures of success.

Society implants hundreds of standards for what you are supposed to have, when in reality, from the perspective of Unity, you are a divine being with access to everything you require, needing nothing.

Not being able to accept the present moment is a sign of resistance and you hit life hard when you resist, such as the rigid tree that receives the impact of a speeding car. When you accept the present moment, the people around you and yourself, you are letting the wave carry you away. True, you may be afraid, but then you will understand that you and the wave are one and the same, and fear will disappear.

So, go ahead and enjoy everything, regardless of whether your mind tells you that it is good or that it is bad. Don´t offer resistance to either. When you feel sad or anguished or in the midst of a big problem, look it in the eye, observe it, talk to it if you can. Say "I am here now and I let you pass through me; I will not resist." Visualize yourself as that flexible or even transparent tree and think of the car as the problem that is approaching at full speed. You will feel that the problem won't crash into you but simply pass you by and speed away.

This is so because the Universe is composed of Yin and Yang energies.

If today you are up, tomorrow you will be down; if today you're happy, tomorrow you'll be sad. The more you resist change, the more shocks you will have in your life, as well as more pain and anguish; you will be stretching the bitter moment. The less you resist change, the more you learn to go with the flow and let things pass without opposing resistance, the faster that unpleasant things will pass and make room for those things you do like.

Enjoy today, the very moment you are living. Be thankful, breath in the instant and stand tall before any situation. Face it and let pass through you. Wait until it passes and welcome what comes next. You have much to enjoy and you may not see it because you are in resistance, but if you stop resisting you will see and be able to smile, experience joy and peace and as a consequence heal your body and soul.

Why? Because the Universe's vital energy will again flow through you, the pure love emanating from the Whole, the love that cleanses all and heals everything. You will go back to a state of equilibrium, of balance and all the words that are synonyms of integral health.

f. Above All, Love Yourself

Our mind judges everything and tells us constantly what is good and bad. Would you like your son to speak ill of your grandson all the time? Or to tell him to bring in his belly or that his hair is ugly or his face too round; or that he still has not managed to earn his first million, nor he has finished a project that he started. We say things to ourselves like: you don't deserve that vacation because you have not been able to stop smoking, nor lose weight; and you continue to have a terrible temper. You have not started saving yet; you can't get a better job, etc. Sounds familiar? Is it similar to your mental noise? We are so cruel with ourselves, so critical!

I think this is the reason why we can't enjoy the present moment and our lives. How can we appreciate a beautiful sunset, even in the middle of traffic, if we are judging ourselves and others all the time? Acceptance requires a measure of love towards the person or the moment that is being accepted.

Accepting life itself requires our love. However, we relate to life from the perspective of judgment and fear, based on preconceived notions; in other words, from the perspective of the ego. In order to accept the present moment, you first have to be able to accept yourself. Change starts within you.

The moment you become able to embrace life with compassion and without judgment, you will be able to embrace the instant you're experiencing. If you feel ready, you may hug yourself tonight, before going to sleep. It may seem difficult, but give it a try. You have nothing to lose! Do it tightly and think of yourself as when you were little. Tell yourself that you are embracing yourself as a sign of Self acceptance, both for what you have achieved and for what you have not.

Accept yourself with the body, the hair and the face that you have; with your temper, your failures and your mistakes. This is a physical way to embrace your whole life. When you see yourself as your inner child, you will realize that you are easy to love in spite of having been abandoned for a long time; in spite of feeling lonely and afraid. You will feel the compassion that your life needs in order to heal.

Think of all the things that you don't like as something that your inner child did or didn't do. Don't be so hard on yourself!

What I am trying to say is that if you can't enjoy the moment you are living perhaps you don't love yourself enough or you lack Self acceptance.
Maybe it would be worthwhile to look into yourself and see what you are still judgmental about, what have you still not managed to accept in you.

My mother used to often tell me to bring in my tummy and I know she meant well. Surely she told herself the same thing and probably heard it from somebody else. I grew up with that idea in mind, plus my ballet teacher used to tell us the same thing. I learned to bring in my tummy all the time and several things happened. First, my posture was affected and the curve of my spine changed. I suffered from back aches which persisted too long in my life, but I also have one leg that is longer than the other and this may have something to do with it too!

Recently, as I finished a session of Chi Gong, the teacher told us to put our hands over our bellies and to caress them in a circular fashion, while we thanked our organs as a sign of gratitude for their hard work during the length of our lives. When I did it, tears sprung out of my eyes. I realized that I had never smiled at my organs; much less thank them, for their work over these forty-plus years.

As I caressed my organs I realized just how thankless I had been. No wonder I suffered from indigestion, gasses, gastritis, hepatitis and other illnesses related to my digestion and organs around the general area of my belly. At that wonderful moment, I understood that even my back problems were related to forcing my belly in at all times, not letting life flow through my stomach, restricting the flow of vital energy by tightening my tummy.

I can't help but wonder how much damage I did myself by trying to live according to ideas based on past notions of how one should look. Ever since, I make an effort go in the opposite direction, that is, to loosen up and not force my belly in all the time. It isn't easy because I am used to my habitual posture, so what should be natural now requires my conscious attention. Thanks to yoga and Chi Gong, this has become easier and now I am letting my belly be what it is, pretty and even perfect as I never thought I would be able to regard it.

Allowing myself to be what I am teaches me to love myself more every day, which makes me enjoy my own divinity, as I embrace my digestive organs and my life.

I invite you to accept this moment, to welcome the present without judgment and without thinking about past and future. Accept your life as it is now, including your present roles in life: mother, father, spouse, son or daughter, employee, entrepreneur, unemployed, rich or poor, alone or accompanied or any other way. Accept what you have not become yet, what you yearn to be. Be honest and sincere with yourself and stop wasting energy trying to be what you are not, while saving that energy to enjoy what you are and what you have.

All that is left of your past are the memories in your mind. The past exists in your mind only.

If something from your past bothers you, it is possible to look at it under a different light, as explained above.

Don't forget that, as background and context to your path, there is Divinity, the Matrix, the All Powerful and it is lovingly at your service. It is always at your side. You may ask for help from that network of love, trusting that the answers you seek will come.

You can ask the Matrix to help you dissolve the traumas, ideas and impressions that are not really yours, so that you can embrace your past and be able to always live in the present; with joy and peace, on the path to integral wellbeing. Maybe you feel shame for the things you did in the past or a present condition in your life. That feeling can also damage the flow of life in your body, since acceptance becomes a challenge under such conditions.

Go to my webpage **www.findpeaceandheal.com** and look for the Meditations section. In there I take you through a guided meditation to clean your inner fluids from the guilt that shame has brought to your organs. Once you let all that dirt out of your body, you can find inner peace and thus heal. Take advantage of this gift and begin your healing process today.

Last, I invite you to accept your spouse or partner, who is a mirror of what you are radiating, your vibrations, and therefore what you attract in life. "Don't try to comb the mirror," one of my yoga teachers used to say. Wanting to change your partner is like trying to comb the mirror, something we all try to do at certain times in our lives, myself included. Once you accept yourself, the images in the mirrors that surround you will look better coiffed themselves.

g. Be Faithful Only to Yourself

A dear friend's story is a good starting point to explain what I am talking about. For reasons of her own, she has a hard time visiting her mother; she says it drains her energy. However, she was educated to do what she should, "heaven forbid" if she didn't. So, she feels the duty to visit her parents often.

Because visiting her mother drains her energy, she is never excited about it; it's just something she has to do. One day I told her to ask her inner Self what it really wanted, something she is not used to doing. My friend, like many other women, lives to please others and often puts herself in the last place.

No wonder her parents and even her spouse, her kids and her job drain her energy! Is this good or bad? It's neither, but to me it would be beneficial for her to learn to love herself first, so she can love others. Our Self love is bound to reflect itself in our love of others like a mirror; it is the law of attraction.

A person who is disloyal to herself is being disloyal to the most important person in her life. If you find yourself doing too many things because they are expected of you, it would be worthwhile for you to consider which of these things really give you pleasure and which don't. Thus, you will be able to decide whether to please yourself or to please others. We tend to be so contradictory that we preach fidelity to others as a moral and spiritual virtue, while we are not even loyal to ourselves. How can we demand loyalty from our partner, if don't practice fidelity to ourselves? This is one of the reasons we are all repressed and full of knots in our bodies. We won't find peace and healthfulness if we betray ourselves all the time.

Another common example of betraying ourselves to please others is when you are invited to a meal and you feel obliged to eat whatever is served out of consideration to you host. However, you may be trying to change your eating habits, increase your wellbeing through the foods you eat.

What is more important, making your host feel good or stop feeling that you are contaminating your body?

Not only are we disloyal to ourselves, but also we strive to control ourselves all the time. We don't allow ourselves to be or do what we want or must, in order to maintain our wellbeing. My more liberal attitude allows people to ask for advice on what to do and this has made me realize how often we want to do things that are restricted by the type of society in which we live.

We tell a boy not to cry, a child to eat all of his food; often we tell them "don't say that" or "don't hit him." When such a child grows up, his subconscious will be full of repressive commands and he will have a hard time stating what he wants or thinks.

A boy may grow up to be a man who does not cry, even when going through a crisis or a serious problem; he will hold back even with his wife. A person will continue to eat everything that is on her plate; another won't be able to defend himself when subject to bullying.

With time, the body of the boy who couldn't cry will cry inside and suffer illnesses. She who eats everything will continue to do so.

He who can't defend himself will lose his Self respect and his sense of security and might even get sick as well. Those who can't speak up may suffer from throat infections or bronchitis. The point is, we get used to living under a certain degree of repression and as adults we have a hard time living otherwise. We have jobs we don't like, relationships that suffocate us; obligatory social occasions and thus we gradually extinguish the flame of our liveliness, which is like being dead through life.

My friends and acquaintances know that I take care of myself, spend time alone and give myself priority in my own life. My challenge is, rather, to make sufficient space for other people. Finding my inner sanity through love and devote myself to those around me is my way to go along my evolutionary path. Some of us abandon ourselves in the service of others, which is Buddha's Compassionate Way, and others forget about themselves and do things against their will, or force themselves to do what is expected of them. We all have to learn to give us the right place in our lives, something we deserve as the divine beings that we are, fractals of the Divinity.

Tantra Yoga teaches us to do the things that spring forth from our being, not only those that are demanded by our discipline or our sense of duty.

So, if one day we don't feel like doing our tantra postures, we shouldn't. Why does yoga teach this? In the path of the yoga, it is understood that it is not good to continue to repress ourselves, even doing things that are supposed to be good for us. We already do too many things because we have to!

Sometimes you refrain from eating something out of a sense of duty. Be careful if this form of rejection stems from your wish that your body be different. Your body feels this form of rejection and when you reject your body, you are rejecting life itself: your life.

Last, I invite you to accept and do all that you want. If you don't do these things for yourself, nobody else will. Be loyal to what you like and respect it above all and everybody else. Give your body rest when it wants; and give it exercise when it so demands!

Don't unduly repress yourself and don't extinguish the joyful nature of happiness and peace within you. Be free and heal once and for all! Rejection and repression block the flow of energy through your body and your life and as a result, toxins may accumulate in your joints, organs and muscles, causing pain and illness down the line. Don't do things because they are good for you, but also because you like them. Do them because you feel like doing them!

4. WAIT AND HOLD YOUR PEACE

a.   Each Recipe Takes its Own Time

How long does an elephant's pregnancy last? Twenty – two months. How long does it take for a business to start yielding profits? Some start right away; others take years. After how many years does a marriage become stable? Some of them take several lives! How long till one can graduate from college? It depends where you start counting.

You can see that each thing requires a different amount of time. You also realize that one does not always know how long a project will takc, but nevertheless you launch it with the expectation of seeing it blossom, one day. Whatever you are asking God or the Universe to grant you will take its own required time. The moment you start wishing for something, your whole being begins to vibrate with the pulsations of that which you are wishing for. Let me give you an example.

When you buy something on line you generate a process in the supplier's network. The supplier takes your order, prepares it, packs it, labels it and ships it; the shipping company then delivers it to your door.
 The van that brings your package has other deliveries along its route and these may take all day. Perhaps your address is the last one on the list because you live the farthest away.

You may get impatient because your order was a Special Delivery and you assumed it would just take a couple of hours, so you call the supplier, complain about the long delay and end up cancelling your order. In fact, you may still want the product, but the delay has upset you. The supplier informs the shipping company of your cancellation and the product is returned to the warehouse.

This is what we do to ourselves when we emit contradictory vibrations. Our lack of inner peace prevents us from waiting for the things we desire. In fact, we don't really know much about the delivery times of what the Matrix is sending our way; we calculate these times by the urgency of our expectations only. When they don't match our desires, we tend to lose control and give up.

Our impatience grows in proportion to our disconnection with the Matrix because when we are connected we don't need anything, since we already have it all. Our yearnings and impatience come from our sense of incompleteness because we are focused on what we lack.

On the contrary, when we are connected to the Matrix we know we are a fractal, which comprises everything; as part of that infinite universal Unity, you may desire things in peace and joy, not with anguish and impatience.

Desire is the engine that moves the world. Without it we perish because we lose our motivation to move forward in life.

Often, desire is criticized for being too mundane and even negative, when in reality it is like the fuel or vital energy rushing through your being to make it move. It would take a whole book to deal with this subject and possibly I'll write it one day, but for the moment I would like you to understand that if you stop desiring you are as good as dead. Desire is a sign of being alive; all you have to do is channel your desires in accordance to the Matrix. Whoever is depressed is unable to experience desire.

Desire is like a spark that turns on the engine of our lives, the oxygen that fans our flames. Our connection to the Matrix and Mother Earth, as well as and the joy and peace which stem from it are like firewood. This combination is the recipe for our liveliness, for our adequate functioning in life and for our advancement.

Each one of our cells requires these same things: fuel or food – protein, carbohydrates, lipids, etc. – water, and the sparks which originate in our chakras, which is desire.

Not living in the here and now also impairs our ability to be patient. Connecting to the present will bring you peace and there will be no restlessness in your waiting times. When you live in the here and now, you can enjoy each breath, each sun ray, your hands, your feet, your eyes; each day, each hour, each minute and each second.

There is no waiting time and in fact time ceases to exist, when you live in the here and now, because life is happening and you find everything enjoyable. Send your wishes and desires to the Matrix in all confidence and enjoy the wait. Let your desires vibrate in the peace and joy of knowing that they are on their way, while you continue to enjoy the here and now and continue to heal.

You will find joy and peace reconnecting with yourself, with your vital energy source, recuperating your Divinity. Active meditation is one way to achieve this and I will discuss it in more detail further down. It is not the only way, but it is a good start and it works for me, which makes me want to share it with you.

What if what you desire takes more than one life? No matter. Continue to vibrate with your desires or you would be sending contradictory signals to the Matrix. Don't cancel your order out of impatience, but continue to speak to the Matrix in the language it understands, which is that of energy vibrations, just like your own.

b.   As You Vibrate, So You Shall Receive

You may have heard the biblical injunction "as you confess, so you shall receive." With time, I learned that while this may be true, what we wish for and what we receive goes beyond words.

Many times we may have confessed and declared positive things and received nothing. Now I understand why. Words are the language of humans, but the Universe understands the language of vibrations. It is the vibrations behind the words that do the work and mobilize the Matrix on our behalf.

For example, when you have financial problems you may feel the anguish that comes from having many bills to pay and no money to pay them. You may cross your fingers and bite your fingernails repeating "I want more money, I need more money, please send me some money."

However, days go by and money does not come your way. What's happening is that while your words say "I need more money" your vibrations are screaming anguish, uncertainty, scarcity and want. Can you see? It is ironic that we vibrate in the exact opposite ways to what we wish to get.

The same thing happens to the person who desperately wants to find a partner. Her words say "Lord, send me a spouse" but her vibrations scream to the Universe "I am alone, how horrible, nobody even looks at me." It doesn't matter whether you ask in prayer or just think about it; all ways are good. What is important is that your words are accompanied by the right types of vibrations, those that are consistent with your desires.

How can you do this, when your subconscious mind may be betraying you? There are whole books that can teach you different methods to vibrate correctly in order to receive what you want.

Understanding that I am the Matrix and that I have no limitations has worked for me. In their book The Law of Attraction, Esther and Jerry Hicks explain the thermometer of our emotions and the vibrations that go with each; it is commendable reading on the subject.

Going back to the example of wishing for money and vibrating scarcity, one of the ways in which you can change your vibrations is remembering a time in your life when there was no scarcity. For example, when you lived with your parents and scarcity was not your problem since they paid the electricity bills, the rent, the phone bill, your education, your food and your clothes. Can you remember that time? Try to go back to that epoch. How was it, to not have to worry about bills that needed to be paid? Now that you have recovered the memory of that sensation, you can send your petition to God or the Universe again.

Fear, depression and grieve are emotions that bring about low energy vibrations and make us feel bad and disempowered. Joy, liberty and love, on the contrary, are emotions that make us feel good and empowered. Obviously, we all want to feel good, so the question is how we can go from an emotion that makes us feel bad to one that makes us feel good.

Esther and Jerry Hicks propose a practical and easy method to convert negative, low frequency emotions into increasingly positive emotions. I'd like to share it with you because it has worked for me.

In the next page, I share with you a black and white graphic of the Thermometer of emotions, but if you want to have a full page, full color, print ready version of this graphic, you can go to **www.findpeaceandheal. com** and get it completely free for you to have it handy and use it whenever you need.

True measurement of what you are attracting to your experience

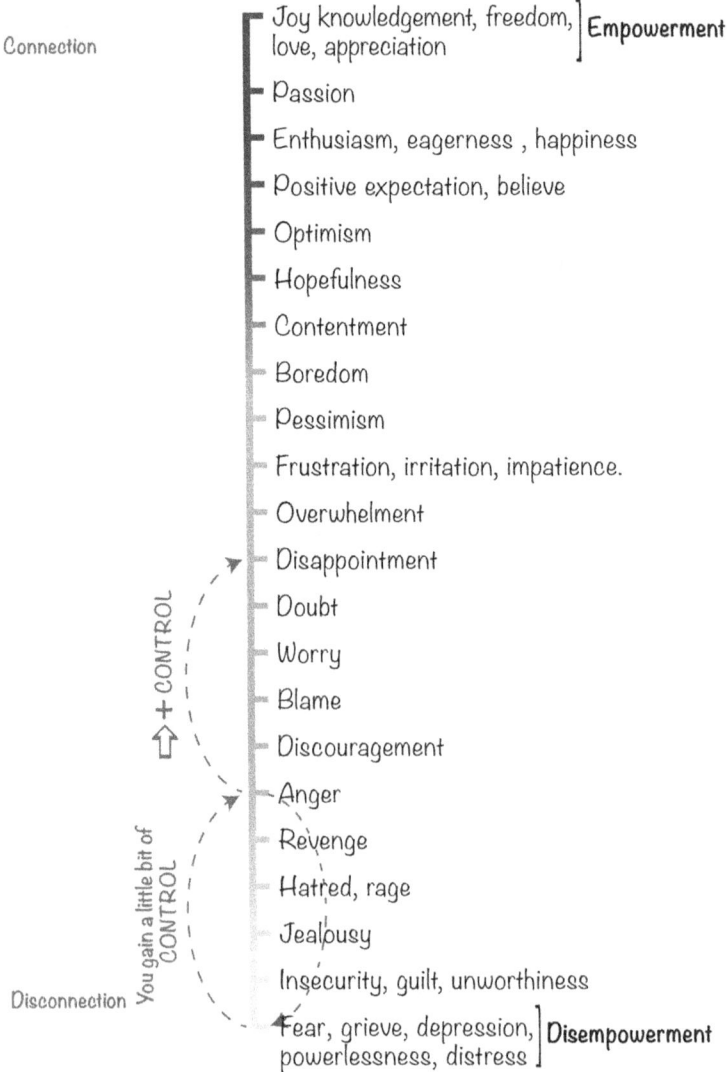

Connection

Joy knowledgement, freedom, love, appreciation } Empowerment

Passion

Enthusiasm, eagerness , happiness

Positive expectation, believe

Optimism

Hopefulness

Contentment

Boredom

Pessimism

Frustration, irritation, impatience.

Overwhelment

Disappointment

Doubt

Worry

Blame

Discouragement

Anger

Revenge

Hatred, rage

Jealousy

Insecurity, guilt, unworthiness

Fear, grieve, depression, powerlessness, distress } Disempowerment

+ CONTROL

You gain a little bit of CONTROL

Disconnection

Figure 5: thermometer of emotions

Make use of this thermometer to go from a low frequency emotion to a more empowering one. In my web page **www.findpeaceandheal.com** I have also included a full color copy, ready to print, free of charge chart where you can see how negative emotions rate very low frequencies and the opposite happens with positive emotions, which rate higher frequencies.

When translated into practical words, if you are at peace, then you have enough strength to do many things, think clearly and help others as well. When on the other hand you feel guilty, you lose your strength to do things. Lower frequencies due to emotions are like little charge on a battery. Here is a black and white copy of it for your quick reference, but I recommend you have one handy for your convenience.

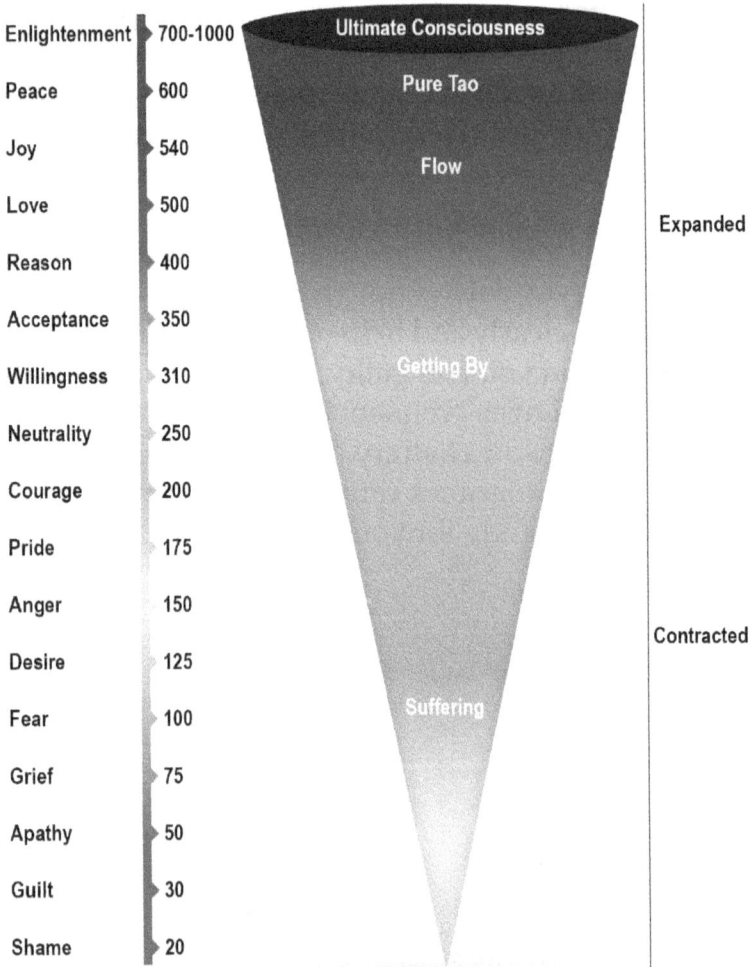

Enlightenment	700-1000	Ultimate Consciousness
Peace	600	Pure Tao
Joy	540	
Love	500	Flow
Reason	400	Expanded
Acceptance	350	
Willingness	310	Getting By
Neutrality	250	
Courage	200	
Pride	175	
Anger	150	Contracted
Desire	125	
Fear	100	Suffering
Grief	75	
Apathy	50	
Guilt	30	
Shame	20	

Figure 6: Cone

Let me tell you a personal anecdote. I used to have a maid who had been working at the house for 10 years. She was an excellent person, good at what she did and I love her a lot, not to say how much I was used to her. However, she happened to have a lousy temper and she was frequently in a bad mood. Persons like her fill the air with negative vibrations, which end up affecting all those around them and I knew she was not a positive influence on me or my family, but for one reason or another I would not get around to firing her.

As I moved forward in my awakening and healing process, it became clearer to me that I had to let her go. This person robbed my peace and that of my husband and daughter, but I believed that I had to learn to tolerate her and that is why I would not fire her.

One day I got mad at her; we quarreled as we often did. Anger coursed through my body like a bitter poison. I felt it clearly that day. I realized that I was taking care of myself, eating right, changing my habits and practicing introspection and yet I was letting myself be contaminated by someone to whom I was paying to be at my service, at my house! What she did that day was the last drop in the glass of my tolerance. However, I did not want to act out of anger; I wanted to come out of that harmful emotion first.

I remembered the emotions thermometer and decided to find the emotion nearest to anger, in order to move up on the scale of positivity.

The first emotion that appeared to me was that of being let down. I remembered all the times I had talked to her in order to try to improve things; the many times I had tried to help the situation, only to bump into her lack of willingness to cooperate. I recalled how many times she had made my daughter and her friends, as well as my own friends, family and visitors, feel bad; the times she had thrown away things that I wanted to keep, etc. I remembered the times she had let me down. In a few minutes, I went from anger to disappointment. This may seem useless to you, but disappointment has a higher energy vibration than anger. From there I went to impatience. When I really want something, I usually get it, so I made a few phone calls and quickly found a replacement, a person I had recently met and liked. She was looking for work and I had found her attitude agreeable. In a few hours I had made a plan to fire my maid.

From the feeling of impatience, I moved to that of hope that my new employee would represent a new beginning.

I would be able to teach her my new eating habits, without undue opposition; she was a more amenable person, who would better cooperate with my family and our other employees. All this brought a feeling of positive expectation and hence enthusiasm. So, in a fairly short time, I went from anger to enthusiasm! My energetic frequency was again at a high level; the poison in me had dissolved and my inner peace restored.

This is an example of using the thermometer of emotions in your favor. You not only need to know the emotions and how they affect your vibratory frequency, but also how to move along that thermometer in such a way as to contribute to your inner peace and your healing process. I am so thankful to Esther and Jerry Hicks for this contribution to humanity, myself included!

c.   Don't Worry, Life Does Not End Here

My purpose in writing this book is not to convince you that other lives exist. Only you have the right to allow yourself to believe whatever you want. However, I can tell you about my own experiences and those of other friends or acquaintances.

Dr. Brian L. Weiss, a psychiatrist, in his book Many Lives, Many Masters explains how he came to accept the existence of other lives and that the present life is just a part of the process of our existence. Reading it changed my perspective on the subject. Now I know that my relative success in this life is the result of the good things I planted in my past lives. I know I have come a long way and this knowledge has helped me find peace and sanity.

When you know that this life is not all there is and that you still have other lives to live you are no longer in a hurry; your impatience goes away and your path seems longer.

Now I understand that some of the things I desire I will get in this life and others will materialize later. My sense of the Eternal has given me peace and toned down my excessive eagerness, as I am no longer in such a hurry.

Impatience is a product of social standards we have accepted as given truths, but they are not absolute truths. Neither are they your own standards and you don't have to rule your life by them. You operate in the perspective of eternity, where time does not exist.

Time is just another perception that constrains our being and I do not wish to be ruled by it. As I said before, you can reinterpret your past to bring it in line with your present and your future. We are used to thinking of time as linear, but if you open your mind and heart this is not necessarily the case. Again, it would take another book to properly address this subject and it is probably beyond my capabilities at the moment, but I would like to share a few examples with you.

Have you ever realized that the seed of a tree has within itself all the information needed to form a complete tree? A tree's entire future development history is all there, but in a latent, invisible state. Could this humble seed introduce itself to you as an oak tree? Why not? Is it not a woman's fertilized egg a living being? If you care to consider it in some depth, the moment a sperm fertilizes an egg, they both cease to exist as egg and sperm and become one forming a new life, which contains all the information needed to develop a person.

Western medicine does not acknowledge what ancestral Chinese labels Jing, or essence. A seed has within it, though hidden, all of the potential transformations, which happen as a plant takes root and later develops and grows, as explained in the Chinese Medicine Compendium, by Erick Marié.

The fact that a fertilized egg is so small does not mean that it is not a new life. Going back to the last question, Is an oak seed a tree or not? Was your son your child the moment you conceived him? If not then, when did it become your son? When you found out you were pregnant, three months later? Can you see how the future of that seed or fertilized egg is also its present?

Your future is happening right now, just as that of the seed. If you look at things this way, everything you wish for may be happening already, germinating somewhere. The fact that it hasn't materialized yet or that others don't see it doesn't mean that it does not exist.

A fertilized ovum is not visible but it is a life already. The mother doesn't care if others see it or not. She only knows she's pregnant and that's sufficient for the life of that new being to have become a reality.

That is why it is so important that you continue to visualize what you desire and vibrate accordingly. Be aware of it, watch it, feel it, live it; enjoy it now as you would a new son. Remember that everything is enjoyable, even if it hasn't materialized yet.

If you believe in a Superior Being, have you ever thought that it is eternal? If you believe this, and if you know you are a fractal of Divinity, then you will be able to understand that you are eternal too. This includes being here and now, as well as in the future and the past, which goes beyond our material existence, ruled by the linearity of time. If you can change your perception of the past, it means that in a sense the past is still happening. You continue to live your past, and so do I. What about the future? We continually live in it working to make it better! We go back and forth in time, don't we? Perhaps this will help you understand the timelessness of your existence and the eternity of being.

So, don't get overanxious if you have not fulfilled all your wishes in this life. Relax, be peaceful. Sooner or later they will come to pass, if you continue vibrating in accordance to them.

d.   Why Not Dream Big, Then?

If you can see yourself as the eternal, timeless being that I just talked about, then you may know that your dreams can be as big as you want them. You are the creator of Heaven and Earth! Do you dare to read this line aloud?

It may be hard for you to accept this now, but this

does not make it less true. Just as the tip of an iceberg, you are part of a self-replicating fractal. Your dreams and wishes can be as big as you want.

I say all this in second person singular, but it is part of a conversation I keep with myself. We all have two beings living within ourselves. Some call them Divinity and Ego; others the Big I and the Small I. To me, they are the Divine Being and the Material Being.

How come the Material Being always wants to be in control? Why can't we be controlled by our Divine Being? If this were the case, all of our problems would be solved! We would not feel jealousy, envy, anxiety, doubt or mental confusion. We would not relate to life from the stand point of fear and thus it would be normal for us to dream big. In fact, our dreams would sooner or later cease to be just dreams, because without fear, our main obstacle, we could make them all come true.

As I explained before, however, we have become disconnected from the Matrix, which is our Divinity. From that moment on, we forget who we are and what our joyful nature is and feel the insecurity of the finger separated from hand I mentioned before. Fear takes over us, giving rise to a spurious self image, which is our ego, our Material Self.

Your ego has no faith in your ability to create a new world. It doubts your Divinity; this is especially true when you act out of anger, despair or in a heavy spirit. Your ego is not your friend.

In the last chapter of this book I will share with you what I know about taking care of your Divine Being. Last but not least, there is no hurry. Take it easy! You have more than this life to achieve your dreams and evolve. You are eternal and therefore you have all eternity. You decide when you want to begin enjoying your joyful nature and when to stop relating to life from the standpoint of fear.

5. ACTIVE MEDITATION

a. Silencing the Mind Is Possible

We have all heard about meditation and the quieting of the mind, which seems like a faculty beyond our reach. No wonder, since we live in a fast, changing world where information travels ever faster. Our minds work just like a smart phone, which has increasingly more windows open to the external world.

Why should we quiet our minds? For the same reasons you turn off your computer every now; otherwise it might get stuck and stops functioning properly. Your mind needs to be silent in order to achieve several vital goals: 1. To listen to the spirit within you, which is your essence; 2. To recharge the batteries of your main power source; 3. So you can stop relating to life from the perspective of fear and do it from the perspective of love or the Divine Being; 4. In order to find the peace, joy and happiness you so much desire; 5. To watch and observe your desires materialize.

1. Listening to the spirit within you amounts to listening to the Divinity, to God and the Universe. How many questions have you been unable to answer today? Would you like to know those answers? It's easy if you realize that all the information of the entire Universe resides within you. There is no better master than you.

The mind is the muscle that we exercise the most in our bodies and as such it has acquired disproportionate importance in our times. It is admired and applauded; a bright mind has become synonymous of superiority. All of this has led us to believe that thinking too much can't be harmful. Furthermore, when we have a problem we often say "I have to think about it;" when we face a difficult decision we also say "I have to think what to do." However, we rarely say "I need time in silence in order to intuit the solution to this problem." We tend to believe more in what the mind tells us than what we perceive through our spirit, without realizing that the mind is the cell phone, the gadget, while the spirit is the sum of all the information that travels through the web. What is more valuable, the gadget or the web?

We adore the creation more than we revere the Creator. We admire what has materialized rather than the creative source from where it sprung. Silencing the mind is a beneficial practice since it puts into perspective for you what is more important and what less. In the silence of the mind wonderful things happen and one of them is that you can listen to the subtle but unmistakable sounds of your spirit. If you think you have never heard the spirit within you let me give you a couple of examples.

Mothers sometimes don't agree with the medical diagnosis of one of their kids. If you are a mother, you may have taken your kid to the doctor several times without noticing any improvement; you might even have changed doctors a couple of times and in spite of following the doctors' instructions it dawns on you that something else is going on. Things are not right. You get the hunch that it is not a matter of medicine but of the spirit; a subtle but distinctive message.

The answer you seek may come to you as simply as through a television program or because you happen to hear the testimony of someone with symptoms similar to those of your child. This gives you a hint to follow in a new direction and so on until you find the right persons, the right advice to cure your kid. In the end you may even realize that your child is perhaps reflecting something that is inside you or in your house; the cause of the malaise may not be physical and you may have something to do with it. It may be your spirit talking to you. We all have it inside ourselves, but some of us cultivate it more than others; some learn to listen to it and others don't, it depends on the person.

Remember that wherever you aim your intentions you will place your energies and therefore that something will grow. What doesn't interest you will not receive your energy and therefore it is bound to not prosper; it will grow weaker and may eventually die. This is part of what I call "active meditation." Aim your attention at that which you wish to strengthen, and you'll see effective results. For example, when someone goes to the gym with the intention of strengthening her arms and sets that as her main workout goal, you will see that she goes regularly and uses the right equipment. This person is paying attention to her arms, looking at the mirror while she exercises and will notice any improvement. The attention she places on her arms achieves a couple of things: i. She brings vital energy to those areas. ii. Consequently, her arms receive more blood, which implies more oxygen and nutrients to the cells, as well as the removal of more of the cellular excrements and toxins.

In an analogous manner, if you pay attention to your child's illness and you allow your instincts to guide you, surely you are bound to find a solution. The Universe may bring the right persons in front of you, or the right medical articles. Even day-to-day events will speak to you with the answers you're seeking. Therefore, place your attention on that which you wish to accomplish, don't neglect it for a second and for sure, subtly but unmistakably, you will get the answers you're looking for. For this you need a little mental silence. If your mind is swamped with the everyday noise of trivial thoughts, these subtle messages will pass you by. If you are always busy with your thoughts, you will not be able to pay attention to the things that truly deserve it. Later we will talk about doing less and how this may greatly contribute to silence your mind a bit, in order to reconnect with your Divinity.

2. Charging the batteries is another way to silence your mind. What happens when you have many applications open in your smart phone and on top of that you are watching a video on YouTube, listening to music and answering your Whatsapp, Snapchat and emails? Your cell phone runs out of battery sooner than a phone that has less applications open. The same thing happens with your vital energy. When your thoughts can't stop their comings and goings, when the things you have to do clutter your mind; when you are full of doubts, worries, memories, suppositions, etc., numberless thoughts and ideas coming and going, day and night, discharge your internal batteries. When this happens, you are like the living dead. You go through life in automatic; you cease to shine and forget about your dreams and your life's illusions. You lack

strength for new projects and can't come up with bright ideas. You get discouraged and in the end get ill, not only in your body but in your soul as well.

It's easy to visualize this if you think of a vehicle. Without a battery, a car won't start. The most you can do is push it and a car is heavy! But when your batteries are fully charged life becomes a pleasant trip, where there is always something new to learn and each day is fresh and full of light.

It's easy to understand using a car as example, but difficult to put into practice in our lives.

Things that distract you are many and sometimes they are so attractive that it really takes resolution to put a stop and pay attention to nurturing your inner self.

That is why you see so many people who look entirely turned off, whose batteries are completely out of charge.

As I said before, your body and your spirit's upkeep is within the realm of your responsibility. Only you can constantly recharge your internal battery in order to transcend in this life and elevate your consciousness in order to enjoy your nature of happiness and peace. You and only you can make the decision to heal.

3. Silencing your mind helps you stop relating to life from the perspective of fear or the ego and enables you to relate to it from the perspective of love, from the standpoint of the Divine Being. The ego is that part of you which keeps shouting "don't do it because 5% of the people who do it may experience problems" or "be sure to buy insurance because 10 of each 100 vehicles have an accident;" "be careful, don't open your heart because you might get hurt;" or "defend yourself because nobody else will care about you." As I said before, the ego relates to life from the standpoint of scarcity and fear. Ego fears everything because it is needy. It can't produce or create anything and therefore it has to take from the rest of your being. It knows itself to be finite and weak. You are a Divine Being since the spirit lies within you; you are a being of light which is trusting as well as timeless. How come the Divine Being has no fear?

A candle manufacturer is not afraid of having no candles at home in case of a black out. Why should Divinity experience fear, being the fountain of love, the creative force behind all things? The Divine Being knows the moment she needs love it will be at her disposal; not only will she produce it but she is all the love there is. The moment it needs to be provided for, provisions will materialize. Only she who ignores her divine essence can feel fear instead of joy, peace and love.

Most of the thoughts that keep us awake at night are worries about the future. When this happens to you just remember that these are notions created by your fears. Remember at that moment the Divinity resides within you, that you are the fountain of love, the source of everything and whether you feel it or not this is a Universal truth that will serve you well. Meditate upon this truth as much as possible and you'll see it become a reality in your life. Your Divine Being will become stronger every day and your fears will concurrently weaken and you will eventually find mental peace. Your internal batteries will achieve periodic recharges, your light will shine and your life will heal.

4. In order to find the peace, joy and happiness you so desire, it is indispensable that you manage to silence your mind increasingly more. The state of Divinity is one of quiet and calm. Obviously, if you are relating to life from the standpoint of fear and its mental noise, anxiety and worries that accompany such state, you don't have too many moments of calm to enjoy everything you have, like children, health, house, family, sunny days, etc. When fear dominates your life, you can't enjoy all you have because it is constantly bombarding

you with its thoughts of scarcity and want. As in a cascade, an occasional good thought is replaced by one that is not so good, followed by a preoccupation which may be the prelude to one of your main worries in life, one of those major things that you feel you still have to do.

This constant bombardment keeps your sympathetic nervous system in a state of "flight and run", in which we breathe rapidly, with our heart pounding, our mind cluttered, our temper bad, our sleep impaired, taking our meals on the run, with our time always limited and our health from bad to worse. This state was designed for emergency situations, as when our ancestors had to escape from a predator when we lived in caves, or to respond to an assault or an attack, or to act quickly in case of a health emergency. When our sympathetic system gets activated we can achieve feats of great intensity; excitement rules, as well as sensorial stimulation, emotional responses and other intense activities. However, even though it is useful, it also consumes the body's energy faster than the body can replace it. This nervous energy is our vital energy.

The result of all this is a depletion or weakening of our nervous system, which these days has become a chronic state for most people in the whole world (*The Tao*

Life by Daniel Reid). On the other hand, the parasympathetic system, or the circuit of rest and relaxation, rules our immune system, controls our self cleansing and purification and our excretory functions.

Our body has evolved to function in equilibrium between these two states of nervous response; total calm comes after intense activity. When we live in the sympathetic mode for long periods, as in the case of modern cities when, a person works at least eight hours a day and then faces one or two hours of intense traffic to get home and do household chores, go over homework, plan and prepare for the next day, there is no time for recovering the equilibrium of body and spirit; sleep is not deep because of the many preoccupations and pending matters. Immune response gets stunted, the body's cleansing and excretory functions get impaired and toxins accumulate in our bodies, paving the way to illness and decline, both physical and spiritual, as Daniel Reid explains in *The Tao of Life*. This sort of life style shortens our lives and departs from our true nature.

Working excessively, abusing food and beverage, over stimulating our senses and excessive emotional stimulus confabulate to maintain our action circuit in the nervous system turned on day and night, which brings the majority of people to a state of chronic toxemia.

I believe toxemia to be at the root of all illnesses, a subject that I would like to address in one of my upcoming books.

For the time being, I want you to realize how indispensable it is to provide rest to your mind and body and that a way to achieve it is through meditation, both active and transcendental, as well as other forms of meditation which propose to silence the mind a bit, to give way to the activation of the parasympathetic nervous system, where you will be able to find assuagement, calm and peace. As I said before, when a computer overloads it needs to be reset, just like the spirit and the body. The mind needs to be quiet in order for calmness to set in. Since our lives are so intense in every way, we belong to a generation that desperately needs meditation, silence and calm, which have become hard to find in contemporary society.

A clogged up person cannot be happy. Look around and watch. A clogged up person breathes rapidly, agitatedly, can barely focus his attention and therefore forgets many things; he eats in a hurry, frowns all the time, stares vacuously, cannot look you in the eye for any length of time because this requires a measure of calmness that he lacks; his ideas are confused, he lacks mental clarity, makes wrong decisions; In sum, he has no peace and isn't happy. One cannot be happy living life as a scared cockroach.

I used to live that way, running here and there, tense, worried, overexcited and without quality time for me and my beloved ones. When I happened to be with them, I was not really there, or just barely. I didn't even have time to pursue my goals and desires and then complained when they didn't come true.

As I mentioned above, for our wishes to materialize we need to vibrate with them, continuously and without contradictions or double messages. What happens when we don't devote a few minutes a day going over our wishes, vibrating in synchrony with them, feeding the flame of our desires in order to let their vibrations go on and expand? Most probably we will forget them and other thoughts and tasks will fill our minds. With the passing of time, we will stop vibrating in synchrony with them and, in my example above, our shipment will be stopped en route, without reaching its destination.

5. One of the advantages of active meditation is that it helps your desires to materialize. I keep a file with all of these wishes written down and well organized, next to my

meditation couch. I really don't call them my desires anymore; I call them my vibrations. I have come to understand that as I vibrate so I express and attract what I wish for. Several days a week, before I do anything else, I devote 15 minutes to reading my "vibrations file," since for the first time in my life I have made a commitment to myself, to vibrate according to what I wish and not forget to do it. Oftentimes I add something to my vibrations list and they become clearer in my mind, my heart and my being.

I know with all certainty that everything we see, which has already materialized, was one day a dream, a vision, a plan. Someone vibrated for it to happen and did it in such a way that it became material life, just as each one of us was created.

That is the way I start my active meditation each morning. I read the list of my desires and vibrate in synchrony with their essence; I enjoy them, I see them, I visualize them, I feel their smells, see their colors; in short, I already live them. By doing this, I make my intentions more concrete. I give direction to my day, my year, my life. I am already living in those places, experiencing those events, fulfilling those purposes.

I stay quiet during those moments, so that I concentrate in vibrating with what I am creating, from my inside out. My mind really enjoys these minutes because I love the film that is projected in my imagination, images that are powerful and full of bravery, filled with joy. It is a gift for me to be able to start my days this way.

Once I have clarified my intentions, I proceed to silence my mind and for that I make use of any of the techniques that I will shortly explain. I have learned them in meditation courses, through coaching, etc. You may find lots of information on these subjects as well.

i. Breathing 4x4x4. This is a simple way to become initiated in meditation. It consists of inhaling deeply during four seconds, holding your breath for another four seconds and then exhaling during four seconds too. And so on. By doing this you are exchanging thoughts for inhalations, holding and exhalations. This meditative exercise will teach your mind to stop in the face of respiration. In the beginning you can breathe whatever way is easier for you, usually in a pulmonary way. My advice is that, with time, you learn to breathe with your diaphragm, that is, with your belly. Think about the way babies and puppies breathe. They naturally breathe using their diaphragm. Nature is wise and perfect and that is why the least conscious of beings breathe this way. Diaphragmatic breathing has many advantages over pulmonary breathing. One of them is that it helps your heart rest from its arduous 24-a-day job. I transcribe the words of Dr. Al Salmanoff on the diaphragm: "It's the body's most powerful muscle; it acts as a powerful impelling pump, which compresses the liver, the spleen and the intestines and stimulates ventral circulation. By compressing abdominal lymphatic and blood vessels, the diaphragm contributes to blood circulation towards the thorax.

The diaphragm's number of contractions per minute is a fourth that of the heart, but its capacity to move blood is much higher because the size of the impelling pump is so much bigger and its force larger. It suffices to visualize the area surface of the diaphragm to realize that it acts as another heart." (In Daniel Reid's *The Tao of Life*). In other words, just as when you milk a cow, the diaphragm exerts pressure over the cava vein, which picks up blood carrying the body's cellular detritus and takes it to the heart and lungs, so that carbon anhydride can get expelled. With the help of the diaphragm through diaphragmatic breathing, we are helping the heart to save great amounts of energy and effort in this process of disposing of cellular waste. Besides, with this type of breathing you recharge your internal batteries with your being's vital energy and that is why oriental philosophy and Chi Gong gives it much importance.

With great joy, I share the link to my web page **www.findpeaceandheal.com**. In the section on Meditation you can find a tutorial to learn to diaphragmatic breathing completely free.

ii. Become the observer of your own thoughts. Breathe deeply whichever way you can – pulmonary at first, diaphragmatically as you get used to doing it – and when a thought surfaces concentrate on observing it. Watch it as though you were just a witness. Observe the next thought surface also. Continue breathing deeply. Just watch your thoughts. Don't get hooked on them.

The idea is to just look at them, don't analyze them, don't build them up, don't get agitated over them, and do not get involved in them. Just watch them. Remember that matter behaves differently when it is observed. When you get used to watching your thoughts you will also notice that between them there is a small space, a trough, a break. This space, though small, is what you are looking for with this kind of exercise, since this space is pure consciousness, a resting place between your thoughts, the calmness your soul so much desires; your body's sanity, the place where you will remember who you are, what your purpose is, as well as glimpse your joyful nature of peace and happiness. Don't lose your patience! You have spent your whole life in a thinking mode, so don't expect to learn to *unthink* overnight. But do start practicing. If you persist, as in everything else, you will succeed and you will soon reap the fruits of peace and joy.

iii. It is important that you deal with the things you have to do in an orderly manner. While we have many outstanding matters and issues, perhaps we could have addressed quite a few of them, or at least gone some ways towards finding them a solution, if we dealt with them with order and discipline. For example, a little girl wants her mother to take her to the movies. They are riding together in the car and the girl sees a poster of the movie she wants to watch. She screams "¡Mom, mom, I want to watch that movie!" The mother answers her "Okay, but not today, darling." The girl insists "But mother, please, I want to. Mom, take me to the movies." The mother could choose to get mad at the girl for her insistence, since she can't take her to the movies at that very moment. She could scream at her and get upset. This is analogous to having a thought surface and paying attention to it, upsetting your meditation practice and interfering with your breathing.

However, the mother may also find a solution to the situation by telling her daughter that she will take her to the movies, but not today. Perhaps Saturday afternoon, she might propose. The mother gives the girl her word and in exchange asks that she calm down and stops screaming, and let their car trip go on pleasantly. If the mother breaks her promise, the daughter will get upset, but if she does take her to the movies she will have gained credibility with her daughter. You can deal with the things you have pending in a similar manner, planning to address them in a concrete way.

Thus, when any of these issues comes up during your meditation, you can discard it with authority, reminding yourself that you have a plan to deal with the matter already and that this is not the time to think about it. Turn the page and go on and if the thought returns breathe deeply and turn the page again until the intruding thought dissolves.

iv. I also advice you not to try to do too many things. For the love of you, try to do less. While the world preaches to do more, I propose the opposite. Remember the old say, "Don't bite what you can't chew." The world we live in has a Yang culture.

Accomplishments are commended over the fact of just being. Material goals are preferred over spiritual ones. One runs a lot, talks fast, breathes in a short and agitated manner and there is no time for anything. Ironically, all these material pursuits are supposed to bring us the happiness we so much yearn for. "I'll be happy when I get my degree," a freshman thinks. "I'll be happy when I marry," thinks the single girl. But it turns out that the young man graduates and is not any happier and the girl marries and soon becomes disillusioned because her expected happiness does not materialize. So, they both continue to do more and more things, believing that any one of them will bring them happiness.

In this rat race after things and accomplishments, one gets so busy as to not have time for silence, for deep, calm breathing and forgets what it is to just be. Doing fills your days and even your future agenda. Your being weakens and when you wish to reconnect your mind refuses to shut up and you can no longer listen to silence, which is the way to your true being.

We are all caught in a world that goes too fast. It is time to become more Yin and balance the equation. True, our Yang side is very valuable and without it we get nothing, but neither do we get anything without our Yin. Just like day follows night, so Yang follows Yin. One way to balance our lives is to do less in order to achieve more.

Think of all the things you do every day and see which ones are superfluous and could be skipped. You will surely find activities that are not really indispensable; some may even be harmful instead of helpful, even if they appear profitable to you.

Remember the rule 80/20, which says that 20% of customers generate 80% of your sales. The same applies to your activities; 20% of them produce 80% of your income or satisfaction.

If you manage to do less and focus on what is truly important to your happiness, your income and your health, you may find time for introspection and meditation, more quality time for the most important person in the Universe, which is you.

Be strict when you go over your agenda. Ponder on what you do each day of the week. If possible, use your cell phone as a reference. There you will find your appointments, the calls you made; remember how you spent every hour of your week.

Our checkbook is another good taleteller on how we spend our time; it tells you where and with whom you were; the same goes for the receipts you'll find in your pockets. At the end of each week, think for a moment about those activities that could be omitted the following week, so that the time you free up may open up space for doing what really matters on your work front, your relationships and the nurturing of your spirit.

b. Live In the Present

We've heard this piece of advice many times and we will continue to hear it. The reason is that only by being present are we truly alive. Statistics say 95 to 99% of time we are not present, but our subconscious mind is taking over in the automatic mode.

The following things happen when you are not present: you get home after a long time in traffic and you don't even know how you got there because you were driving on automatic; your partner asks you about something he'd mentioned before and you don't know what he is talking about because the first time he said it you were not really there; a whole week goes by and you realize that you haven't looked at the sky; you feel that time flies and that's the way it is because you are not there. You were and you weren't.

When you practice being more present, you notice that life is nicer than you thought and also less difficult.

I'll give you an example. As I said before, my mother in law has been living at home for the last couple of years and I knew that my father in law would come to live with us sooner rather than later because my husband is an only son. For most anyone, having her mother in law living at home may sound like a great burden, let alone your father in law as well. It so happened that all of a sudden my father in law came to stay with us for a protracted period because of a sudden illness which required medical care.

He lived alone but his health deteriorated. When he came straight out of the hospital to our house we were truly happy because we had feared for his life. Days went by and everything seemed to be getting back to normal.

We did have to find a little extra time to take care of him, talk to him, give him his medication and personal care, etc. Now, with the benefit of a few months' hindsight, I realize that everything has turned out alright and flowed as it should. When you are able to feed nine people you can stretch it to 10. I was able to focus my attention on what had to be done every day and my new situation was nothing short of enjoyable.

To be present is to flow with the moment; neither get too far ahead nor act recklessly or create too many expectations; to just be in the moment, in the here and now. For the first time, my father in law could spend time with my children and they got to know their grandfather. Before that, since he lived far from us, communications were mostly by telephone and only with my husband and a little bit with me. We had never shared jokes after dinner; nor had we played cards together; we didn't even have pictures of him with the kids.

I am not trying to brainwash you; all I am saying is, if you give all of your attention to the cup of coffee that the person in your care wants and prepare it the way he wants it, if you consider it a joy to take care of someone you love, relish the fact that you do have a cup of coffee to give him, you will not want to miss all these things, that are happening in the present, thinking about the past or the future.

Your life is happening right now, is a phrase I often repeat to myself, so don't miss it!

When I hear my kids shouting or playing their music too loud; when I hear them screaming at each other or fighting over something I tell myself "Don't miss it, Vivian, because your life is happening right now" and nothing repeats itself in just the same manner at the same precise instant in time.

I'll say it again: it's all about being here now. The air you breathe, your lungs functioning, your senses alert, a new day, your family, your loved ones around you, animals and plants, the sky, the rain; I could go on ad infinitum! All is present in the present. It's as though the movie of your life was playing right before your eyes and you were a spectator. All things become magical and their existence acquires new meaning. There are no worries; in the present, everything is alright. When we manage to connect to the present, even heavy traffic seems like a gift because we become capable of enjoying the trees in the streets we're crossing, the splendor of the sky, the night, wonderful music, and our bodies' sensations.

I encourage you introduce the present into your life and enjoy the trip; it is magical and you are the leading character in your movie and at the same time a privileged observer.

Being in the present is assuming a meditative posture in life. Past and future are history and possibilities, but not your own, ongoing film. This is part of what I am talking about when I refer to active meditation.

c. Emotions Versus Feelings

Many times it is difficult for you to be in the here and now because you have perpetuated situations from your past; perhaps you have victimized yourself and even if you don't admit it you now love suffering more than your joy. Whoever experiences a loss, such as a loved one or a sentimental breakup, surely will feel the pain and will go through the inevitable mourning period; he or she may forever miss the person that is gone. This mourning period is necessary and healthy, but impermanent. Skipping it may cause future emotional conflict and damage. However, human beings tend to create attachments to just about anything. Just as we cling to life, which is a good instinct, we also cling to people, places, things and situations.

We learned attachment at home, with our parents, and therefore we are afraid of loss. We don't see change as part of a normal and even beneficial process, but as something bad, to be resisted; and we suffer just to imagine a loss of any kind.

Having attachments is an intrinsic part of our over strengthened egos. Remember that ego is synonymous with fear and egos are afraid of losses.

Why? Because egos know they cannot create or produce anything and therefore they are needy; losses scare them because they don't know how to replace whatever they lose. Their nature is greedy and clingy. As a consequence, when you experience a loss, if your ego is too strong you won't get over it and you will cling to the feeling of loss, to the pain, thereby perpetuating this feeling by turning into a permanent emotion of loss or pain. You become a victim of circumstances.

An emotion is a feeling that has managed to become permanent. It's easy to perpetuate painful past events. We carry within us emotions that may cause us damages. Emotions are like stagnant water inside. Down the line we may experience pains that we attribute to occasional illness, without any relation to our emotions. Those pains and illnesses are related to your inner being, your psyche, emotions you carry inside and have perpetuated by not letting them flow. The more you pay attention to a painful event from the past, the more it will get condensed or materialized.

Since its vibrations are related to pain, anguish or sadness, they have low vibratory frequencies and therefore they weaken you and make you sick.

When you experience the pain of loss, don't oppose any resistance to that feeling. Things pass like water in a river because everything is energy. What you resist persists.

Stagnant waters rot and harm whatever lives in them, killing what was healthy once. When you don't resist a feeling, it passes and sooner or later you will feel fresh torrents arriving to your stream, which will renovate you and teach you life lessons that will make you stronger. These new tributaries will show you that all change is good, that everything transforms itself and in so doing is beneficial to you.

On the contrary, if you resist feeling the pain, this feeling will turn into constant suffering. Feelings of pain are healthy; don't resist them, live through them and let the turbulent waters pass. It is emotions and suffering what you can avoid. You don't have to live in suffering, which is the equivalent to living in stagnant waters, where life rots.

Wise Chinese masters knew from antiquity that matter doesn't get destroyed, just transformed. We have heard this law of nature, but let's analyze it from the perspective of our personal lives. Zhang Zai (1020 – 1077 CE) postulated that the great vacuum was not emptiness at all, but a continuation of energy (Qi) and that this energy's condensation gave rise to all phenomena in the Universe (*Fundamentals of Chinese Medicine*, by Giovanni Maciocia).

This means that each new born being is energy condensation, such that it became materialized, a dense body. It also means that every being that dies (as we call the parting from this world), in reality just transformed itself into a more subtle form of energy and then dispersed throughout what we call the vacuum. All that is subtle and pure, says Lie Zi (300 BC), a great Chinese philosopher, rose to the sky, and all that is heavy and turbid solidified to form the Earth.

A beloved person who, according to your perception, died in reality was transformed into a state of original purity. This great truth of nature may free you from suffering from the person's death. All those who have taken their subtle form are still alive, dispersed and free from the material world, but living still. In part, we cling to material forms out of ignorance and fear. Get rid of those ideas, which tie you to the past and feel free to come back to the present, to your Divine Nature of joy and peace, of constant change, beneficial transformation and permanent evolution.

In sum, to be able to live in the present you need to detach yourself from the past that you have perpetuated. Only by being in the present can you enjoy a way of living that is meditatively active, which is a way to heal inside and out.

Plenitude, joy, peace and well being take place in the present time. I bid you to live your feelings to the top, each one at its corresponding moment; cry when you have to and laugh anytime you can. Live your life with intensity and don't cling to anything or anyone. Let the waters flow and heal yourself inside out.

d. Connect with the Universe, with Mother Earth and with the Heart of Humanity

No electrical gadget or machine can function without electricity or batteries. You are a perfect machine and as a part of your perfection you need vital energy to function in life. Without it, you're condemned to die as the last drop of your vital energy is spent.

You happen to have such a battery system inside yourself. Let's compare the functioning of the brain with that of the mind. The brain is a physical organ in charge of vital functions, while the mind allows you to think, reason, order your ideas and perceive your feelings.

Blood circulation brings nutrients to each cell and takes away excrement and in so doing bring energy to the cell. Have you ever wondered what is more important, nutrients or oxygen?.

If you look at it carefully, you will easily conclude that oxygen is more important to our existence than food itself. Without the first, you die within a few minutes whereas without food you can go on for days and even months. What is the content of the air we breathe which makes it so vital?

Ancient spiritual masters, philosophers and sages have given it different names; Prana, Qi (Chi), Breath of Life, the Holy Spirit and so on. The breath of life, the Qi, brings life to the Being. Without it there would be no one alive. A common way to determine if someone is still alive is to ascertain whether the person is still breathing. Oxygen carries the Qi, the vital energy I am talking about. In other words, with each inhalation you recharge your internal batteries and gain increased vitality.

Breathing recharges our internal batteries. However, most of us don't know how to breathe adequately. We only know how to breathe in and breathe out, automatically, responding to signals from our nervous system. But there is much more than just inhaling and exhaling.

Ordinary breathing keeps us alive so we can perform our day to day activities, but it does not contribute much to recharging our internal batteries.

In my web page **www.findpeaceandheal.com**, on the Meditation section, I teach you how to breathe appropriately, so you can take advantage of therapeutic and spiritual benefits of diaphragmatic respiration. For now, it is enough that you understand the fact that breathing is a way to recharge the internal batteries of your vitality, of your life, since respiration connects the body with the mind and this is exactly what we do when we meditate. Note that I say mind and not brain. That is, I am talking about a material activity that connects the dense and physical with the spiritual and subtle, two which are the same but we have separated. Both mind and body rely on vital energy; it is the battery in the machine and without it nobody can function.

When you manage to remain in mental silence for any length of time breathing deeply, just as I said before, is as when you recharge your cell phone. Certainly the batteries recharge. If you don't interrupt the recharge time, you will have battery for a long time. This is why meditation is so important.

During meditation several wonderful things happen; one of them is that you reconnect with Mother Earth and the Universe. In case you haven't heard it, Earth is a source of negative energy and the sky a source of positive energy.

Taking this into account, the traditional meditative posture is sitting down with your back straight, so that energy from Earth and sky can freely flow through your spine and you can recharge more efficiently. Energy flows from your spinal column to the rest of your being; through the nervous branches through your central nervous system, which connects the brain with the periphery of your body; to your vital organs and tissues, through what are called the meridians, which have distributors along the spine; and to the main chakras or transformers, which are in charge of reducing the frequency of subtle energies that enter our organism, to make them usable by body and mind (Reid, Op.Cit.)

What happens when a light bulb gets positive and negative energy? Voilá, it tuns on! What do you think will happen when you constantly devote time to meditation, breathing deeply and silencing your mind for periods that become longer and longer as practice allows? Of course, your life will light up. You will have energy, vitality, joy and strength to achieve all you wish.

Daniel Reid says that the spine is the stairway to Heaven, since it connects earthly energies that stem from the ground to cosmic energies that come from the sky, transforming them to frequencies and patterns that may be used by the human energy system.

Last, I would like to add that our batteries get recharged in a setting of silence. Each time we speak, what comes out of our mouths is pure internal energy. Think about each word as though it were an energetic burst that springs from your inner source, from your reservoir of energy, from your internal batteries. If you talk a lot, surely you will have a harder time being silent. In my case, it's been a real challenge to keep quiet for longer periods of time, but when I understood that with each word I spoke my vital energy came out and got dispersed in the cosmos, it became easier.

These suggested practices require a degree of self control, discipline and awareness. With the determination to achieve your goal of peace to heal, however, you surely will accomplish this, sooner rather than later. Don't get discouraged when you catch yourself engaged in a senseless conversation, judging someone else or talking too much. What is important is that now you are aware of it, whereas before it went over your head.

As Daniel Reid says, silence is golden. This led me to see that there exists within me a source of pure gold, which is my vital energy, from which I depend. As of that moment I take care of it, caress my belly and meditate everyday with the awareness and intention to increase my reserves of internal vital energy and not waste it on empty words.

Active meditation includes breathing deeply and slowly, keeping your back straight and being in silence, both in words and in your mind. All of this is to achieve a better recharge of our internal batteries, so that your reserves increase and not diminish. If you devote each day of your life to this beautiful internal work, you will become, as my master of Chinese Medicine and Chi Gong Ernesto de Leon says, a millionaire in energy; your days will become longer and your old age dignified and with good health.

e. The Observer

One of the objectives of active meditation is to make you the observer of your own acts, thoughts, feelings and emotions. Realizing that most of what you do, say and think is not you, but your acquired ego is something I have emphasized all along. You will see how wonderful it is to be able to detach yourself from that invented character and start to be your own true self, become your Divine Being, your essence. What you do, say and think you are is not really you but a character you have invented, a costume you put on every day to act on the world's stage. Beneath that costume hides a divine being and that being is Divinity itself; all of the information, the light and the truth.

You can look at your life in two ways, if you compare to a drop of sea water. Either you think you are just that, a drop of salt water, or you think that you are the entire ocean contained in a drop of water. You are the entire sea contained in a single drop; all that exists is within you and you are everything. That is why those of us who believe in the Unity as a universal law and in the Tao say that we are the One (God) and the One (God) is us. We know that the entire ocean is contained in a single drop.

By becoming your own observer, you will understand that the things you do and say everyday are not you but your acquired self, what you have been programmed to be, your ego, your preconceived ideas, what you think you are supposed to do and say. The more you observe this character, the better you will be able to unmask it and the more you will see beyond that being to find your true Self, the pure consciousness that is you, the divinity of your essence.

This is another benefit of meditation: the more you practice it the more you will be able to find the divine being within you and the more you will become detached from your acquired self. As a result, you will find the inner peace and the integral healing of your body and mind that you so much desire.

ABOUT THE AUTHOR

I AM

I really am I AM!

I was able to understand that I am the Whole and the Whole is I.

When you wake up to this great truth, your perspective on life will drastically change.

Perhaps you have heard the phrase: "God is in everything and fills everything;" This is what I am talking to you about. I am the I AM, experiencing the world and this life from the perspective of Vivian Baak. My name only serves to identify me and to provide a reference to the life experience, whereby that great I AM produces this book and its webpage **www.findpeaceandheal.com**.

I am 43 years old, married with a son of 14 and a daughter of 10. Both my parents are alive. I have three sisters, one brother and six nephews and nieces. My mother in law lives with us at home. I can say that I have plenty of good company!

I am a lawyer by profession; a fashion designer, a businesswoman, a writer and most of all, a Healer.

This book and all of its contents are the result of the aforementioned awakening and are witnesses to my transformation. I am very thankful for all I have lived prior to this stage, since it brought me to this point. I know that this evolutionary process does not end, that it goes on and on forever. For the time being, I enjoy sharing with you and the world all that has been revealed during my periods of introspection and what my teachers have taught me.

My intention is to contribute to your evolutionary process, so we become the Unity that we are, and together grow and heighten our consciousness and propel our world towards a future of abundance, joy, integral health and peace.

For advice, conferences, radio and TV shows you can contact me at vivianbaak@findpeaceandheal.com

Welcome to our world of light.

I AM, from

Vivian Baak

REFERENCES

Chapter 1

Page 1   www.enbuenasmanos.com

Page 2   Ho´oponopono, by Ulrich E. Du prée

Page 3   Adapted from Ho´oponopono

Chapter 3

Page 3   The Law of Attraction, Esther and Jerry Hicks

Page 6   Dr. Brian L. Weiss, a psychiatrist, in his book Many Lives, Many Masters

Page 6   Chinese Medicine Compendium, by Erick Marié

Chapter 5

Page 7   The Tao of Life by Daniel Reid

Page 7   http://findpeaceandheal.com

Page 13 Fundamentals of Chinese Medicine, by Giovanni Maciocia

www.ingramcontent.com/pod-product-compliance
Lightning Source LLC
Chambersburg PA
CBHW072004060426
42446CB00042B/1823